MW01674023

Written by Betsy Bass
Paintings and Artwork by Betsy Bass

Published by Wild Lark Books

Wild Lark Books
513 Broadway Street
Lubbock, Texas 79401
wildlarkbooks.com

#supportartreadbooks

First Printing, 2022

Poetry | Paperback | Inspirational
ISBN 9781957864617
Bulk orders can be made directly through the publisher.

eBook Available
ISBN 9781957864624

MESSAGES AT MIDNIGHT

Note from the Publisher

WILD LARK BOOKS

Wild Lark Books is an independent publisher that supports authors as artists.
As with all works of art, reviews help build readerships and increase the impact of the artwork.

If Betsy's writings and artwork have inspired you, please help support her artistry by leaving reviews online, sharing about it on social media using the hashtag of the title (#messagesatmidnight), or speaking about it to all of your friends.

Your support would mean the world to us.

Thank you!

Wild Lark Books
Support Art. Read Books.

Learn More About the Author at
WILDLARKBOOKS.COM and BETSYBASS.COM

Messages at Midnight

BETSY BASS

WILD LARK BOOKS

18 May 2022-2:48 am

Dedication: To all who create, appreciate, and radiate beauty

Contents

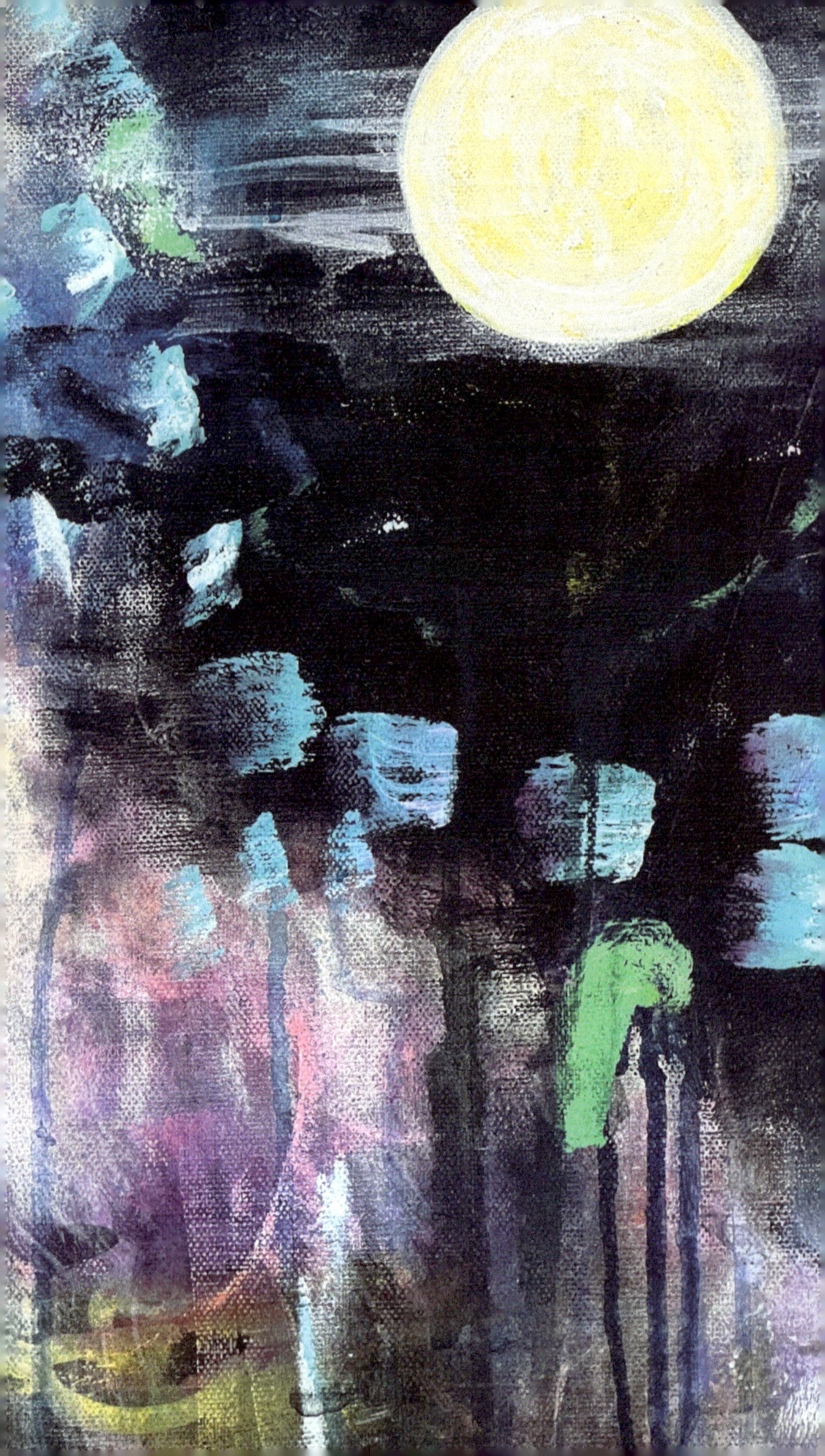

Introduction

Many people write a book because they have an experience to share, some wisdom to impart, or a story burning to be born. I never set out to write a book, but I opened myself to a connection with the Divine, and poetry started pouring through me. In 34 nights, I downloaded 102 poems, sometimes being awakened as many as five times a night. Some people asked me if it was difficult and suggested that I ask the Muse to visit me during the day, but I decided that I felt fine receiving inspiration in the middle of the night—and since I always fell back asleep easily, it was not a problem for me.

At one point, I became worried because I didn't understand what was happening to me, and I wanted the poetry to continue beyond what I was given. My ego intervened, and I was afraid that somehow I would jinx the process and cause the whole experience to disappear. I learned to accept the concept of ambiguity, and I never did understand how or why it was happening.

Giving up control was part of what worked for me. Not having a goal for the gift allowed me to be more receptive and less directive about the entire experience. I believe that the process of surrender allowed me to be in flow.

After downloading the poems at night by hand, I typed them the next day so that I would not be overwhelmed and fall too far behind when I received poems the next night. I was surprised at the depth of the messages. Consistently, I received thought-provoking, encouraging, positive messages for living a full, creative, joyful, spirit-led life. Several weeks after the poems stopped coming, I decided it was my job to share these messages with the world. A year later, I published *Spirited Poems for Spirited People*, which contained 49 of the 102 poems organized into seven categories: inspiration, exploration, imagination, restoration, transformation, unification, and celebration.

This second collection of poems continues with themes of hope, love, creativity, connection, playfulness, and openness. I have been delighted to learn that the poems in *Spirited Poems for Spirited People* have encouraged people and made them feel seen, heard, and understood. We all need to be witnessed. Often we are so influenced by outside voices that we can no longer hear our own. Using this collection of poetry as an oracle is one way to tap into your own inner guidance and intuition. As Robert and Hollie Holden share in their Course in Miracles community *Everyday Miracles 2022*, "get quiet, settle it, and invite in your own inner teacher." You will be guided to select the right poem with the wisdom you need.

My prayer for you is that you find peace, love, joy, encouragement, and a sense of belonging as you discover your own meaningful messages in *Messages at Midnight*.

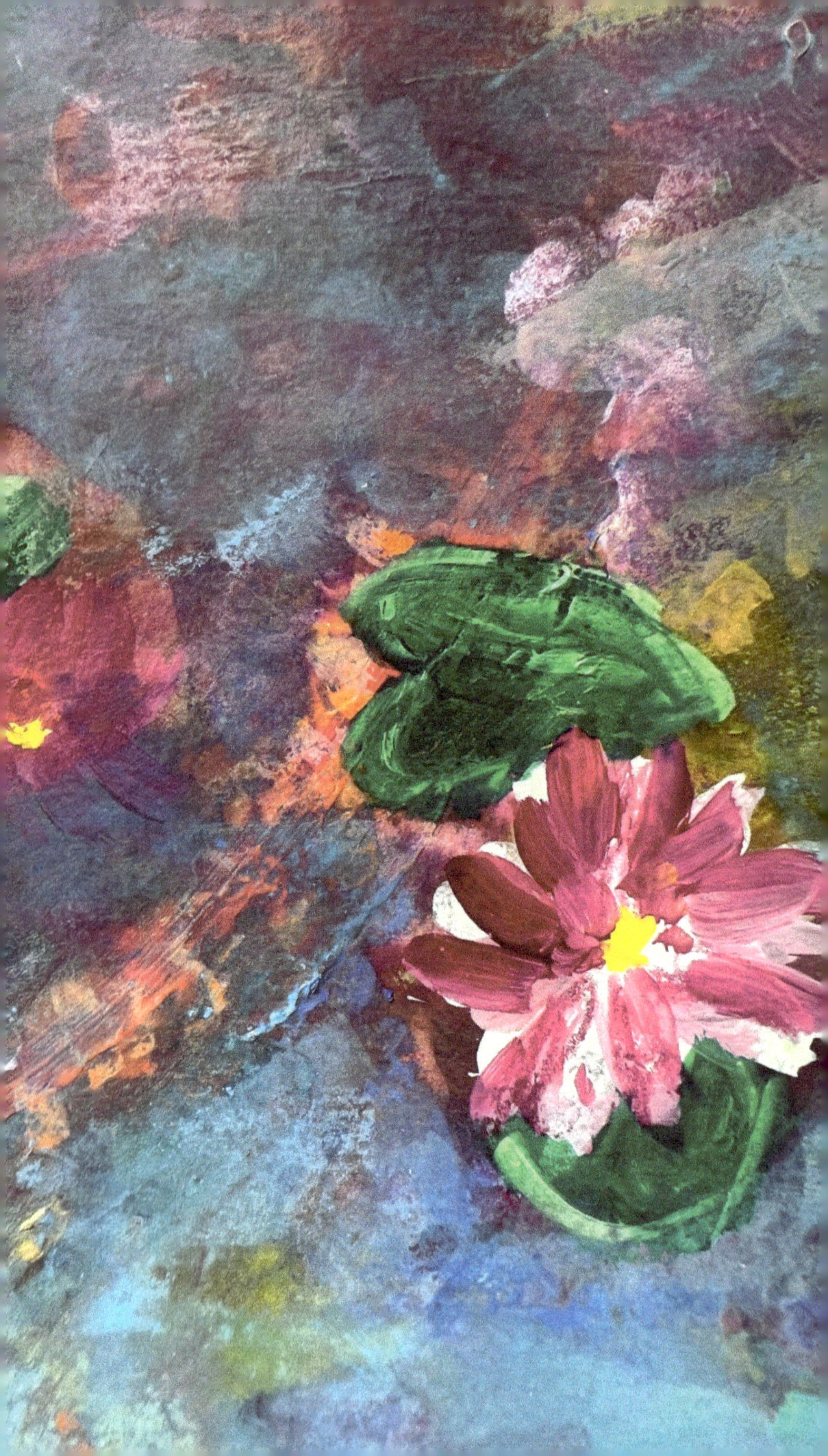

Meditations

Spinning

Started at 1:43 a.m. and finished at 2:25 a.m.

Are you spinning your wheels or
spinning around in circles
as you get dizzy with the effort but go nowhere?
Does the spinning cause you
to feel disoriented and confused?
Are you spinning like a top
as you careen across the floor?
Are you spinning so fast that your head hurts
and you feel nauseated and confused?

Sometimes you get into motion with
no real plan for where you want to go.
You start in one direction and seem to
lose your way as you crash off into another.
Strange forces intervene, and you ricochet
like a billiard ball, hitting all the corners.

Sometimes you spin because

you like movement, or you procrastinate
and don't do what you said you would.
Sometimes other people knock and bump you,
and you're not sure you like it.

Maybe you cause others to spin.
Do your unkind remarks
cause someone to spin off in
unproductive or unfavorable ways?

If you're cognizant that you're spinning,
and you want to stop, that's a start.
Notice and become aware when you wake up.

Look around and notice your whereabouts.
Instead of spinning around the room as you
collide with others and make yourself sick,
reflect upon the question: Do I still enjoy spinning?

Perhaps it's a habit, and you think
there's no other way.
Now that you notice you've been spinning,
you have the gift of awareness.
You are no longer asleep in your life.
You survey your surroundings.

"Do I want to spin here, or is it time to spin
in a new neighborhood with a different crowd?"
You may continue to grow in consciousness
and wonder if you're spinning in a direction

that still holds meaning for you.

You may realize that you want to spin
opposite from the direction you've been traveling.
You rarely look around and take a breath.
You're not much of a spinner,
and you prefer stillness.
You got set into motion years ago by
someone else, and it never occurred
to you that you could choose to stop.

It's your responsibility to take a big breath,
open your eyes wide, fling your arms out,
and open your heart.
Do you still want to be spinning,
and if you do, for what purpose?

It's okay to change.
Change is one of the only
things you can count on.
Nature is your teacher,
and it changes all the time.
You can reassess and decide if you
still want to define yourself as a spinner
or are you ready for a novel role,
direction, or plan?
You don't have to know what you're going to do.
Take a break, make an assessment,
switch directions, or stop if you want.

If you're waiting for permission
from someone else, it's not going to happen.
This is something you must do for yourself.
Go inward, get still, invite in God
and your spiritual team.
You're never alone, though you
may feel that you are.
Breathe, pray, be still, and listen—
not just with your ears,
but with your entire body.
What feels right for you now?

You may continue to spin, and
you may be a world class spinner,
or you may discover that you
ended up in a job, family, or
location that doesn't fit you anymore.
You may discover that you were
never really cut out to be a spinner.
Maybe you're a glider after all.

Careless

Started at 5:27 a.m. and finished at 5:37 a.m.

Are you careless with
your commitments
and careless with
your words?
Are you careless with
your promises?
Are you careless with
your time, your friends,
and your soul?
Are you careless with
your thoughts, actions,
and hopes?
Are you careless
about exercise
and your need
for self-care?
Are you careless
with friends and

with the need to befriend
yourself as well?
Are you careless
when you drive,
when you talk,
and when you pray?

Where is your attention
and what really
counts with you?
Do you spin
your wheels and
waste your
time on projects
that don't matter?
Do you know what
your heart wants or
are you careless when you
try to figure that out too?
What could you do
to care more?
Sit down, get quiet,
take a breath.
Don't ask an expert,
but go deep within the cavern
of your own heart,
the true seat of
wisdom and knowing.
With a big exhalation
of stale energy and

yesterday's thoughts,
ask deeply what you want.

If you're careless with
your thoughts and
race around in your life,
you won't know the answer.

Stop being careless and give
yourself the greatest gift of all—
being with yourself.
You will learn what lights you up,
so as you ignite the spark of
your soul, others have a chance
to turn their light on too.
Everyone needs more care,
not more *care less.*

Sidewalks

Started at 4:59 a.m. and finished at 5:15 a.m.

What are sidewalks for, anyway?
Sometimes they're bumpy, lumpy,
and cracked straight through
from the bulging tree roots
that dare to push sunward.
Sometimes sidewalks challenge you
since they're broken apart and
difficult to navigate.

But sidewalks give you
a space to draw chalky
pictures and hopscotch grids.
You can stroll without worry
that bikes will mow you down.
You can push a baby in a stroller
and have peace of mind.
You're safe from traffic
and able to meander like

a tourist in your own neighborhood.

Sidewalks are a luxury.
They keep you from getting
splattered with mud, but
you might take them for granted.

Do you think about the people
who planned the sidewalks?
Do you remember the laborers
who sweated and poured wet concrete?
What about the artisans
who smoothed the surfaces?

You are one with them,
part of the same fabric of life,
but you usually focus on differences
and what keeps you apart.

You're all woven as part of life's tapestry.
Various threads combine together
to make a huge wall hanging,
a grand piece of art.
God is the artist.
All threads are required
to make the scene complete.

You need the light pink,
smoky gray, rich brown,
vermilion, cerulean,

burnt umber, sienna,
vibrant red, blazing orange,
turquoise, royal blue,
purple, lavender, sunny yellow,
olive green, copper, silver,
gold, navy blue, white, and black.
You need all those colors
to make God's tapestry of humanity.
It wouldn't be the same if
some color was missing.

He designed it all, and it makes sense,
but we take it for granted
sometimes, like the sidewalks.

Trash Cans

Started at 1:09 a.m. and finished at 1:29 a.m.

Trash cans are a
necessary part of life.
They're useful and
help you clear away
what you no longer need.

Does the trash can
care about its purpose?
Does it wonder how
it's doing, if it has
fallen behind, or if
others like, approve,
or even care about it?

A trash can is just what
it was cut out to be.

Why do you make

it so difficult to
be yourself?
How can you be
so confused about
yourself, your purpose,
and your personality?
You find this challenging
because you lose touch
with your essential self.

Somewhere on the journey,
you cover yourself with
make-up or fashion,
jealousy and doubt,
demands or commands
of others, and you
lose your way.

You aren't sure
what you like or
where you want to go
or what you want to do
because it's been so long
since you've paid attention
to the stirrings of your soul,
the desires of your heart, and
the deep call from within.

You bury the small voice
and true wisdom beneath

obligation and resentment,
duty and discretion.
You don't hear yourself
anymore because it's been
so long since you've listened.
You get lost and drop your keys.
You stumble down the path
and can't find your way home
anymore because you don't
recognize what you want.
You put tape over
your own mouth and
muffle the screams within that are
trying to get your attention.

You ignore yourself so long
that it's normal to forget the little
discomforts and urges within
that nudge you toward your soul.

How do you get so disconnected?
Is it the pull to please others,
the quest for fortune and fame,
the need to be noticed, the desire
to be better than others?

How can you make it so confusing?
Why don't you trust and embrace
the truth of who God created you to be?
How can you make it so complicated?

Rest and breathe, trust and listen,
and fill your cells with life-sustaining
oxygen to form a big bubble within
that you can fill with your own
luminous spirit and its swirly,
twirly colors, innocence, hope,
playfulness, and pleasure,
with the chance to say a
big *yes* to life; no hesitation.
You dive right in and know
that if you breathe, make space
and trust, you will know
your usefulness. And like
trash cans, you can just be yourself,
and it will be perfect.

El Tiempo es Ahora

Started at 6:04 a.m. and finished at 6:11 a.m.

Qué podemos hacer si
no tenemos que pensar?
Solamente caminamos adelante,
siguiendo el corazón.

No es importante
saber lo de que no
podemos conocer primero
porque Dios es el
patrón, el comandante.

El decide y da las direcciones.
Nosotros somos los instrumentos,
los juguetes, los objetos como pelotas
en el juego de fútbol.

Podemos aparecer en todas partes.
No tenemos que estar preocupados.
No tenemos que saber o predecir el futuro.
Solamente tenemos que estar listos,
listos para sorpresas, listos para aventuras,
listos para la llamada de Dios.

"Vengan, vengan mis queridos.
vamos a jugar."
El tiempo es ahora.

The Time is Now (English Translation)

Started at 6:04 a.m. and finished at 6:11 a.m.

What can we do if
we don't have to think?
We only walk forward,
following the heart.

It is not important
to know about what we
can't know first
because God is the
boss, the commander.

He decides and gives the directions.
We are the instruments,
the toys, the objects—like balls—

in the game of soccer.

We can appear everywhere.
We don't have to be worried.
We don't have to know or predict the future.
We only have to be ready,
ready for surprises, ready for adventures,
ready for the call of God.

"Come, come, my darlings,
let's play.
The time is now."

Circus Elephants

Started at 12:39 a.m. and finished at 12:59 a.m.

Just like circus elephants who
used to entertain the crowds,
you created your own entertainment,
but now it's not enough.

Circus elephants used to
be adored, cheered, roared,
and applauded, but now
you know you were misled.
You thought it was fine, and
you didn't know any better.

Your life mirrors that now.
What used to be applauded,
cheered, celebrated, and
fine, no longer is.
You didn't get it right,
but you didn't know better.

Your old way reflects insecurity,
self-deceit, posturing, comparing,
cajoling, and pretending you knew
more than anyone else.

You don't, and you never did,
but you thought you were separate,
special, and better than some.
Everyone is in this board game
of life together.
Your moves affect others',
and theirs affect yours.

It was so much easier
to pretend you were separate
little islands, never touching,
never needing to pay attention.

You're all intertwined, and
your lives are inexplicably
woven together in intricate
spider webs of purpose and design.

What you do, what you think,
and how you act reverberates
out into space, setting up
vibrations that are felt far away.
You want your vibrations
to create harmonious melodies,
not cacophonous, discordant sounds

that fall harshly on eardrums.
Remember that what you think
and what you say touches everyone.

Are your notes dulcet tones
or wildly mismatching sounds
with no hope of being a chord
you want to hear or play?
The words you speak are
pebbles dropped into a pond,
forming concentric circles
as ripples move outward.

Are the pebbles you drop
little polished stones,
tumbled agates, amethysts,
smooth flat stones, speckled ones,
or sparkly crystals?

If so, their beauty can unite
people in love, kindness,
positivity, and peace.
Your words and actions
mean something.
You are not just for
yourself anymore.
You are part of one large
matrix of interconnecting pieces,
facets of a diamond,
a reflection of the

hologram of our lives.

What you say, do, think,
and project matter more
than you know.
Now that you know,
you must choose.
Choose to be peace,
love, goodness, and purity.
Choose for the planet,
and choose for yourself.
You can't pretend
you don't know now,
just as you know the truth
about circus elephants.

Freedom

Started after 4:48 a.m. and finished at 5:28 a.m.

Are you really free?
Free from worry and
free from doubt?
Free from anger and
bitter feelings that
eat you up inside?
Are you free to soar,
swoop, and sail through life?

You were created by God
to be free, to live in the
garden of gardens with
Her so you flourish and grow,
not wither and die.

How does freedom feel?
Would you be afraid
if you could fly out

over the trees and
explore without limit,
feel the wind in your face
as you race towards
thrilling experiences?

Would freedom allow
you to slow down, rest,
and rejuvenate your
weary soul and body?

Would freedom mean
you finally leave the job
you don't love to follow
your real passion?

Would freedom allow you
to connect with your
lonely inner child, make it
your best friend so you do
what makes your heart sing?

Would freedom give you
the chance to change
your personality, shed
a negative way you
look at the world,
and stop judging
and feeling judged?
Choose to see with the eyes

of your heart, which
are more accurate.

Would freedom allow you
to be kinder towards others
and more forgiving of yourself?

God doesn't require perfection—
so boring, constricting,
contracting, and controlling.

Freedom allows you to
be yourself and encourages
you to give the gift of
freedom to others, so that
they may also shine their light
which will be different from yours.
When you combine your light
with the light of others, all souls
blaze brightly together to reflect
peace, harmony, and love.

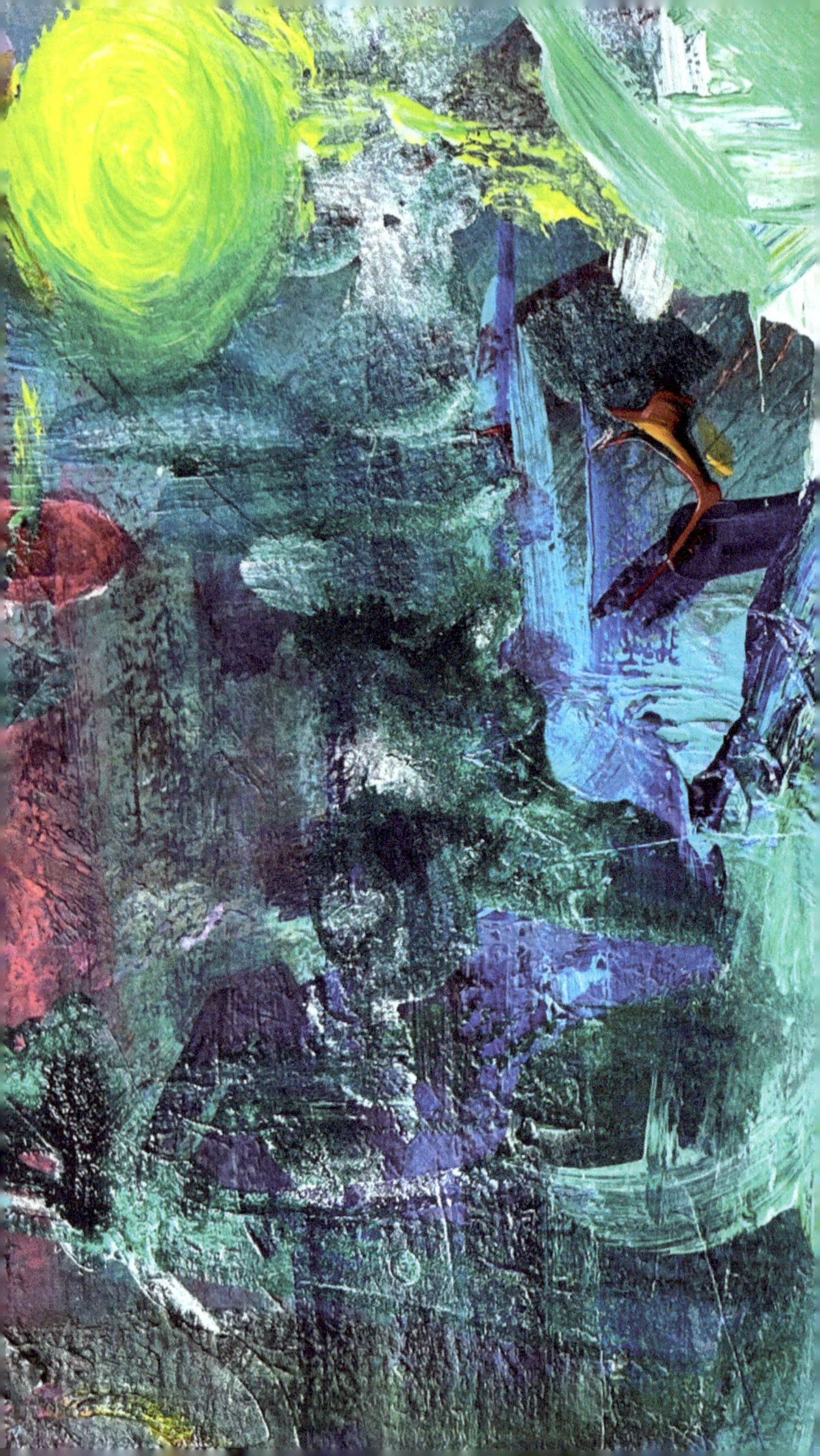

Mirrors

Are You Fancy?

Started at 11:50 p.m. and finished at 12:03 a.m.

Are you fancy in
the proud way you
express yourself?
Are you fancy with
your creativity,
as you let it blaze
a colorful trail?
Are you fancy in
how you see yourself?
Does your own
individual style burst
forth with uniqueness?

Are you fancy in
how you feel about
yourself, as you
delight in your spirit,
shine your light, and

beam a captivating smile?
Are you confident in
who you are and what
you have to offer?

Are you fancy in
the way you allow
yourself to dress,
walk, talk, and learn?
Are you in love with
your bubbly spirit, as
you allow the
reins to just be?

Are you fancy because
you love yourself,
like yourself, and
enjoy your own company?
Are you fancy because
you know you're okay
just the way you are?

Are you fancy like
a three-year-old who
shimmers with self-love,
self-acceptance, and joy,
and who dares you
to join in her fantasy
of pure delight?

Are you fancy because
you're free to learn and
pursue new things,
and you're not afraid
to make a mistake?

Are you fancy because
you know that even
without gorgeous clothing
or pretty jewelry,
you are enough?

Just your love,
just your spirit,
just yourself—
you're fancy enough
for you, and because
you reflect that, you
help others know that
they're fancy enough too.

Balloons

Started at 5:15 a.m. and finished at 5:35 a.m.

What kind of balloon are you?
The shiny mylar one
that pops up, perky enough
to last for weeks?
Are you Batman, Ironman,
Mickey Mouse, or Spiderman?
What about Moana,
Elsa from *Frozen*, or
any Disney princess?

Are you a puffy number
like five, six, or seven?
What about a birthday balloon,
bright with confetti
and warm wishes, which
surprises and delights
your friend, who seems
too old to enjoy a balloon

but loves that you remember
and acknowledge him?

Are you a lover's balloon
declaring eternal devotion
for Valentine's Day?
A love balloon can bring
a smile to anyone's face,
and will delight any
day of the week.

Are you a "Congratulations!" balloon
as you shower attention and affection
on a friend or coworker for a job,
big raise, or celebration of life?

Are you a graduation balloon,
festooned in streamers as you
float above the crowd and
wear your school colors?

Are you a baby shower balloon
that adorns a mailbox,
doorway, or fence as you show
guests how to celebrate,
toast, and honor new parents?

Are you a balloon that
escapes, flying high
above the clouds,

getting smaller and smaller
until you're a speck in the sky?
Are you like that red balloon
in Paris as you travel high
above the city, look down
below, and deliver delight
and hope to observers
who desperately need a lift?

Are you part of a vibrant bunch
that thrills the *feeling-forgotten*
older person who lives alone
but now feels love and inclusion?
Are you a surprise birthday balloon
that dances and darts as your
ribbons get mixed up
with the others?

Are you a balloon for a
new restaurant or business
that bursts with pride
and can't contain your happiness?
Are you part of a parade, theater,
party, amusement park, or
anywhere else you come together
to be children again?
When you join in the magic
as you suspend your take
on reality, you realize that
you too can soar like a balloon,

delight a child, lift a spirit,
surprise a friend, or join together
to mark a special occasion with joy,
love, hope, and childlike wonder.

What can you learn from balloons,
and which one are you?
I want to be all of them,
so you choose first.

Title

Started at 1:09 a.m. and finished at 1:19 a.m.

What would your title be?
Are you a book, a poem,
a song, a podcast,
a movie, or a series?
Do you know?

Are you a comedy,
drama, documentary,
or animated cartoon?
Are you here to entertain,
educate, or elucidate the truth?

What is your title?
Is it engaging and creative,
sexy or sweet, or
surprising or trite?

What do you stand for,

and what stands for you?
Are you here to help, agitate,
or make others grow?

How do you serve, and
who is your audience?
Will they know you
by your pat answers
and rehearsed speeches,
or will you engage others
as you captivate them
with your authenticity,
audacious spirit,
and vulnerability?

Will you be stuck
in your head,
as you try to impress
or use the latest hashtag
on social media?
Will you be real, broken,
beautiful, and flawed,
perfect with your cracks,
so the love and
light shines through?

Is your title dull,
boring, or caught up
in victimhood and excuses?
Will you surprise, excite,

and fill your life with adventure,
or will you calm, help, comfort,
reach out, and inspire?

It's all up to you.
No one else is going
to give you a title.
It's not their job
or their business.
Your title is up to you.
You get to come up
with the message
and the medium.
What do you want
your title to be?

Fighting

Started at 3:48 a.m. and finished at 4:09 a.m.

What are you fighting for and
what are you fighting about?
Do you fight to be heard,
seen, or treated with dignity?

Do you fight for what
you think is right?
Are you fighting because
you were wronged or
is fighting the first
go-to in your toolkit?

Are you fighting for
someone else, some cause,
some other way?
Are you fighting to hurt,
harm, or lash out at someone
who has betrayed you?

Are you fighting to
establish a boundary or
create respect for yourself?

Fighting is not wrong, but it
may not be the best way.
Your anger, fire, piss and vinegar
go out into the universe,
kaboom with intensity
and negative emotion, and
set off other fires of rage.

Feel what you need to feel.
Ask the fight in you
what message it needs
to deliver, so you
may be enlightened.
Feel your emotions in motion
as they move through you.

What is the end goal
that you want to reach?
Look at what's missing and
what you don't have,
so you will know
what you want and
what kind of relationship
you want to create.

The fighting does not

have to go, not while
you learn and discover
what you need to know.
Natural law states that
as you ignite the fire
of a fight, you set vibrations
into motion that draw more
fights and anger to you.
When the fight is over,
get very quiet.
Sit in the ashes and embers.
Then you may discover
a gift, a message,
a kernel of truth
you need to know
about the fighting.

Will You Join In?

Started at 1:01 a.m. and finished at 1:20 a.m.

Will you join in the music,
the art, the parade?
Will you say *yes* when
the group passes by?

Life is a celebration,
and you're here to
live it, express it,
feel it, and be it.
Will you join in?

Do you think that
you're not ready?
Are you under-prepared,
overly concerned,
out of sync,
and not in step?

Why do you wait?
Do you think there is
only one right way?
Your way is the right way.

Don't look for perfection;
participate.
Will you join in?
The music grows louder,
time approaches, and
you can feel excitement
in the air.

Will you join in?
Are you unsure,
unknown, unaligned?
Every voice and every instrument
creates a symphony of diversity.
You need melodies and
counter melodies, a bass line,
a soaring descant,
and driving percussion.
Do you worry that
you won't sound good?
You don't know how
you contribute or where you
fit in the jigsaw puzzle of life.
You don't need to know yet.
What are you waiting for?

Believe in your heart
and know in your body
that you matter.
The gift within you grows
because you planted the seeds,
and the sun of your discipline
and the water of your desire
has nurtured them as they
get ready to bloom.

Trust that you will know when
and where to share the gifts
of your creation.

Why do you wait?
If you wait for approval,
adulation, appreciation,
and affection, it may not happen.
Know that heavenly forces
help you bring forth your gift
and share your talent.
Will you join in?

The world needs your light now.
As you beam your radiance out
without knowledge of how it
will be received, you stir courage
in the hearts of others.
Will you join in?
What you do for yourself

you really do for all.
Didn't you know?
We're all one.

Showing Up

Started at 6:05 a.m. and finished at 6:14 a.m.

How do you show up for yourself?
Are you someone you trust?
Do you follow through
with what you say?
Do you believe in yourself?
Do others believe in you?

Do you take yourself
seriously, but not so seriously
that you forget to have fun?
Do you show up for yourself
in little ways and big ones too?

Do you honor your need for reflection,
meditation, and prayer?
Do you respect yourself and
keep promises when you
commit to write a book,

paint a picture, run a race,
call a friend, do the laundry,
clean out clutter, or
research a new project?

Will you listen to yourself,
or are you out of integrity?
Do you honor your time,
set boundaries, and
ask people to respect
your requests?

If you abandon yourself,
don't think someone
will rescue you.
Show up and stand up
for yourself, and then
others can join you.

Worthy

Started at 6:22 a.m. and finished at 6:31 a.m.

Do you wonder
if you're worthy
to do the work?
Will you take a risk
and not know
what you're doing?

Do you question if
you're worthy to receive
the dream or inspiration?
It's not about being worthy.
You're worthy just by
being an open vessel
so you can receive.

You have to be willing
to catch the story as it
flies by or record the line

of poetry before it drifts
downstream to another dreamer.
If you hum a tune, get up,
and write it down before
the wind whisks it into
the willing ears of some
other artist who will capture it.

Whether you feel worthy
or not is not an issue
because *everyone* is worthy—
worthy of goodness, joy,
beauty, and truth.
You too are worthy of
all of these things.

Worth is not the question;
willingness is what counts.

Are you willing to take
the time to tune in, receive,
record, and remember?
You are worthy, so spread
your intoxicating creativity
out in the world and inspire
others to find theirs.

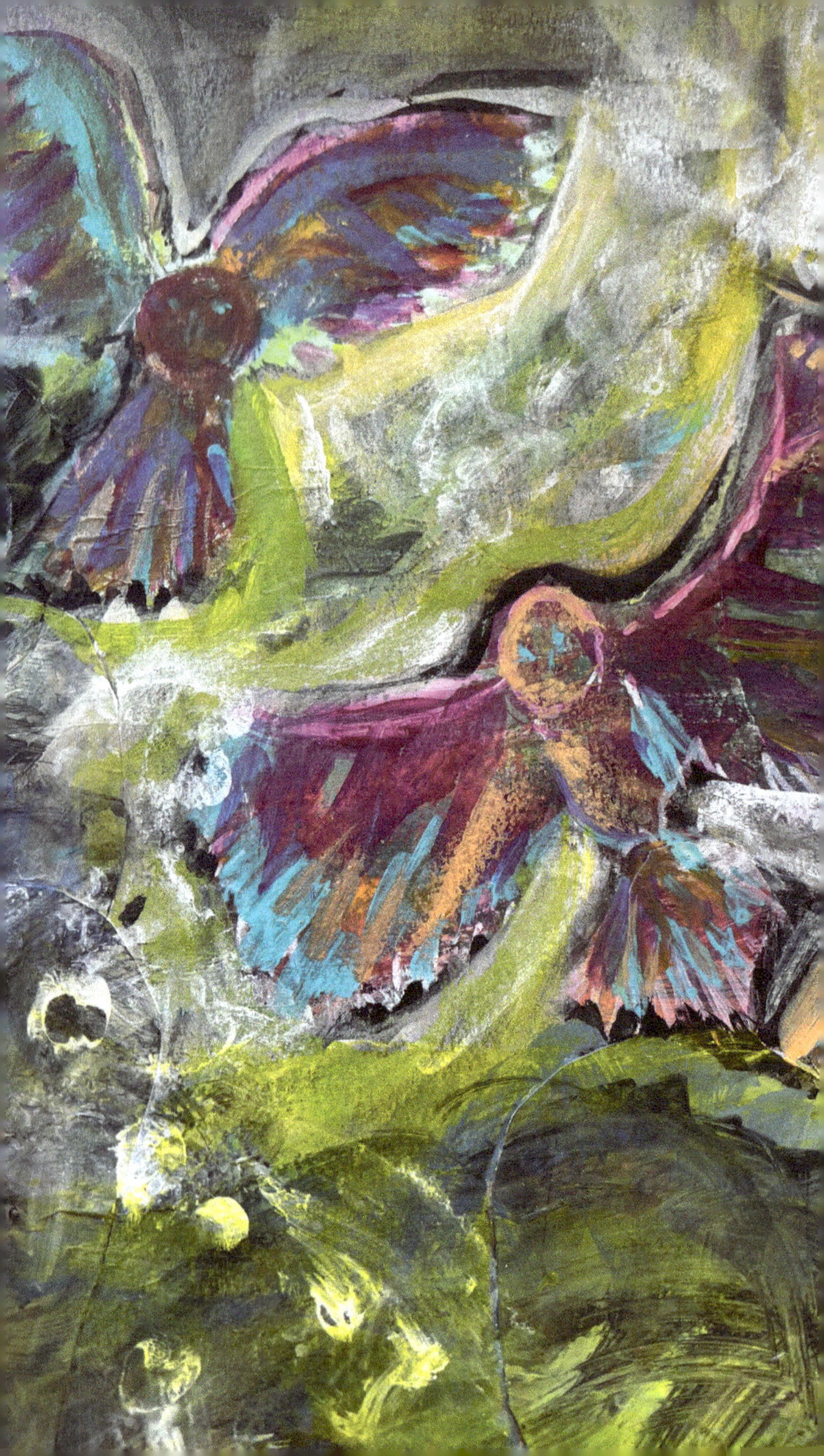

Musings

Farewell

Started at 4:16 a.m. and finished at 4:35 a.m.

When do you know that
it's time to say farewell?
How often do people
overstay their welcome?

When you're ready
for a novel experience,
do you cling to old ways
because they're familiar?
It's easier not to change
what you're doing,
so you go back and forth
in the same rut.

When does your heart
sing out for change?
Are you reluctant or
do you leap at it as

you embrace the new,
the different, the unknown?

How do you know what
the adventure will be?
You can't know ahead of time.
All you feel is a willingness
to put yourself out there.

Will you choose to be a
beginner once more?
Wouldn't you rather be
good at something,
appear experienced,
and act confident?
Unfortunately, unless you get
out of your comfort zone,
you won't grow very much.

When was the last time
you allowed yourself to
be a little kid and decided
to do something fun,
crazy, or exciting?
When was the last time
you checked in with
your spirit to ask if
it felt intrigued?

Sometimes out of

boredom or routine,
you fall back into old habits
or you don't challenge yourself.
What are you attempting
to create in your life?

Do you care?
If you're feeling
edgy or uncertain, you
may be on to something.
Changing a pattern is
not always simple to do, and
when people are presented
with an unknown version
of you, they may prefer to
put you back into a box or
force you to wear a label—
don't let them!

Only you can decide
what feels right for you and
what makes your spirit sing.
Saying farewell to the old
ways may be challenging.

Saying farewell to old friends
may seem odd or uncomfortable,
but if you stretch and grow,
the old you may give way
to the ever-evolving edition.

What is it time to
say farewell to now?

The Way

Started at 6:21 a.m. and finished at 6:38 a.m.

Do you think you
know the way?
How can you tell?
Is it clear to you,
so that you believe
you're never alone?

Help and guidance are
always available to you.
Do you know the way,
show the way,
or become the way
for someone else?
Many people need help and
would love your assistance.

The way is already inside you.
You may be caught

in a loop where you
do the same thing
over and over and
expect different results.

You forget the fun
of the unknown,
when you wander
through a foreign country,
stop at what delights you,
and feel free.

When was the last time
you didn't have to
know the way
but trusted that it
would appear to you?

You may worry that you
won't know the right way,
the proper way,
or the best way.
There is no one way.
There is *your* way.

You can receive guidance
and be led, if you allow it.
Watch for signs, clues,
spirit animals, nudges,
and urges of your soul.

First, discern what you want.
Feel deep into your soul,
belly, and heart.
How will you feel when you
get what you think you want?

Feel the joy, breathe in the relief,
flood your body with excitement.
Believe what you desire happens.
Allow no doubt to seep in.
Create a safe space in
your heart for your dream,
and fill it with childlike wonder
as you wait for a miracle.

You don't have to know the way.
God Herself has a more
magical way than yours.
You may not understand
the best way before you begin.
Let the way be a mystery.
In your heart of hearts, don't you
love a surprise anyway?

Rebirth

Started at 12:48 a.m. and finished at 1:21 a.m.

Despite the winter weather,
you can experience rebirth.
It doesn't seem logical,
but rebirth is a state of mind.

Rebirth is when you have hope,
a fresh outlook, a new lease on life.
Rebirth is becoming yourself,
redesigning yourself, or
finding yourself for the first time.

What does it take to
experience a rebirth?
A willingness to let go.
Suspend beliefs as they
once were, have faith
in God, and trust that
all is right with the world.

It's breaking apart and
dismantling the old way of being.

Rebirth is personal,
and it's an inside affair,
You can't hide it.
Others will notice.
They will see your
renewed sense of self,
your confidence,
and your radiance.
They will be drawn to
your authenticity and
pure delight in self.

Your soul reflects your beauty.
As your wisdom increases,
you will age backwards.
You will be older,
but you will emanate
youth and exuberance.

A bounce in your step and
joy in your heart increases
as you fall into the Divine and
know that you are loved,
led, and guided.
Your joy is God's joy, and
She does not require you to suffer.
She does not ask you to wear

sackcloth and ashes and grovel
as an unworthy one who
can't approach the throne.

God asks you to find
the divine spark within.
Light up your own life as you
love, live, create, and
experience joy and
mirth along the way.

If you look for jewels,
you will find them
in unexpected places:
in the flight attendant's kindness
on a terrible plane trip home
to your mother's funeral;
in a stranger who pays
for your coffee;
in your granddaughter's
funny joke or newfound
sense of confidence;
in a laugh with neighbors;
an unexpected meal
a friend brings when
you feel sick;
in a special thank you
note from a colleague who
tells you she looks up to you
and that your words inspire her.

The gems you discover along the journey
might be the delicious granola
your friend shares with you or
the box of lush pears at Christmas.
It might be the perfect gifts your son
mindfully selects for you at the holiday
or your daughter's loving inquiries into your health.
It might be your daughter-in-law's delightful laugh.

It might be your friend's support as you
blast off into unknown creative territory.
Her encouragement and appreciation keep you
going.
It might be your spouse's gentle touch
or passionate embrace,
A fellow seeker might share
life adventures, work, and insights.

There are many examples in everyday life
when you can experience rebirth,
if you're open to the concept.

Do you need to leave your job?
What about the place you call home?
Are you open to a rebirth of ideas
and challenging perspectives that obliterate
everything you think you know for certain?
Are you afraid to change your mind,
change your job, change your habits,

or give up what's not working?

Rebirth is not for the faint-hearted.
If you're in touch with your true essence
and know you're a child of God,
that you are both loved and love itself,
then you just might be ready
and available for rebirth,
and it's not even spring yet.

The World

Started at 6:28 a.m. and finished at 6:53 a.m.

The world is a fascinating place.
What is the world?
A physical planet?
A huge group of people?
Languages and cultures?
Natural wonders?
Ideas, businesses, and people?
Political concerns and global issues?
All of these are parts of the world,
but your inner world is the most
important world because that's
where you have the most impact.

Things may happen to you
that you would not select,
but you can always choose
your reaction to them.
Don't be a victim in your life.

Your reaction, attitude, and
vibration affects the whole.

Challenges and disappointments
occur, but if you're open to how
you contribute in some way,
you may feel more powerful.

Tragedy, abuse, unfairness.
betrayal, illness, death,
mistreatment, financial ruin,
isolation, depression, and anxiety exist.
You don't want them, but sometimes
you invite them in because
you focus on what you fear.

The more you concentrate on fearful things,
the more you magnetize them to you.
It's best to leave those fears
with God and the angels.
Remember that God loves you
and always tries to reach you.
Your soul whispers messages to you,
and angels brush you with their wings.
Be quiet and still enough to hear.

When your inner world focuses on
divine connection and being led by Spirit,
synchronicities tumble into place.
Populate your inner world with

loving, peaceful thoughts, and
less anger, fear, judgment, and angst.
Invite in peace.

Create your inner world as a sanctuary
of stillness, goodness, and unity.
Your own power can make a
difference in your world.

Reach

Started at 4:27 a.m. and finished at 4:41 a.m.

Will you reach for the stars or
do you stay and orbit around
yourself in a dull, ho-hum life?
Will you reach for the unknown,
the unfamiliar, the new?

Will you be brave and get
out of your own way and
try an unfamiliar dish,
a different friend, a novel way?

What are you afraid of anyway—
that you won't get it right?
Then you'll learn something,
and others will watch and learn too.

Will you reach for the stars,
the moon, the heavens?

Will you lunge beyond the known
and venture out where you've
never before traveled?

Will you seize a dream
and stretch for stardust?
Will you expand and get
uncomfortable as a beginner?

Will you thirst for knowledge
and try unfamiliar technology?
Will you meet different friends
and experience other cultures?

Will you connect with a hurting friend,
assist a neighbor who needs a ride,
counsel a child who needs patience,
guidance, or another chance?

Will you reach out to a person
who wounded you long ago and
be willing to forgive but not forget?
Will you reach out to an estranged friend
or family member to explore a way to salvage
a relationship that once had meaning?

Will you reach and keep your mind growing,
expanding, and wondering so you
don't get bored and become boring?

It's easy to think you know it all.
You've traveled enough, and
you know the way when there
are thousands of ways and
many things you'll never know.

Will you be brave enough
to reach with others?
Sometimes it's easier to
reach out, reach up, reach across,
or reach in if you don't have
to reach by yourself.

Will you be someone's witness
as they will be yours?
If you do, who knows what
you will set into motion and
how far your reach will be?

What Now?

Started at 3:55 a.m. and finished at 4:18 a.m.

You ask what's next?
The feeling of *What now?*
may appear out of nowhere.
Perhaps you start
like gangbusters, but
then you lose your way.
What Now? you ask.

Perhaps you're certain
about the promise of
friendship or love
in your life, but now
things are complicated,
and you're not sure anymore.
What Now? you ask.

You land a new contract,
start a different job,

write the first chapter,
and then, something is off
and nothing seems right.
What Now? you ask.

You begin a course,
sign up for a class,
but it's not smooth sailing,
and you don't belong anymore.
What Now? you ask.

You have your life
mapped out, and plans
are complete, but you
take a detour,
and it feels right.
What Now? you ask.

You plan your dream trip,
make deposits, and
pay for tickets, but
uneasiness gnaws at you.
What Now? you ask.

You choose the best career,
finish the program and
earn a prime position, but
it seems lackluster and
your energy evaporates.
What Now? you ask.

You create a course,
teach online, or host an event,
but learning magic tricks
captivates you, and
your passion catapults you
into a different universe.
What Now? you ask.

You want to write a book
start a product line,
and make a sale, but
you feel like a salmon
swimming upstream.
What Now? you ask.

Get into your boat and
turn it downstream.
You don't need to
know the way or have
all the plans first.
If you're rigid and
unyielding, you may
miss the signposts
along the way.

Life is not meant
to be one neat package
wrapped with a bow
or a pre-planned journey.

The most fruitful and exciting
adventures pique your curiosity.

You will find subtle guidance
from angels as they
show you another path,
project, or passion.
Ask questions, pay attention,
and follow the
nudges from within.
You don't need to
have all the answers.
It's better if you don't.
Then you are free
to create and repeat—
What Now?

Photographs

Started at 1:24 a.m. and finished at 1:46 a.m.

Photographs are a moment
in time, a frozen reality.
One minute you're here,
and another you're there.
Does the photograph of you
reflect your essence?
Do you notice a smile
or observe a frown?

Do you see a soul
living on purpose
or are you discouraged,
fearful, fractured, or facetious?
Do you recognize
yourself as you
beam your smile
and share your sparkle?
Do you vibrate with the

truth of your essence,
or do you airbrush
the photograph to look
more perfect than you are?

Did you do the inner work
so your outer attitude
reflects joy and truth?
Did you grow weary
and think that makeup
or a great haircut
conceals the real you?
When you don't do
the work or create the space
for your spirit to shine out,
then no number of
photography tricks
will make you better.

You can't fake it.
Despite the bright colors
in your hair or wild earrings,
no amount of distraction
covers up fear-based talk,
poor self-control, or the
negative rut that keeps
growing until the hole
you're in feels bottomless.

You may not wear designer clothes,

but your heart and bright spirit
burn with true beauty and your essential self.
Will your photograph reveal a brave,
precious spirit who yearns to be true
to self and won't compromise belief?

Will you express yourself fully and fairly
and not worry that you don't look perfect?
Will the photograph show eyes full of
love, patience, and kindness
as you gaze upon others
as one big family rather
than as splintered factions?

Will the photograph capture
your courage to be fully
yourself in all your emotions,
as you struggle to be
both human and divine?

When your spirit is in charge,
you radiate beauty.
As you grow, change, and share
your vulnerable self, you
encourage others to believe
that they are enough too.
True beauty reflects your heart
and soul through your eyes.
This is the photograph
you need to share.

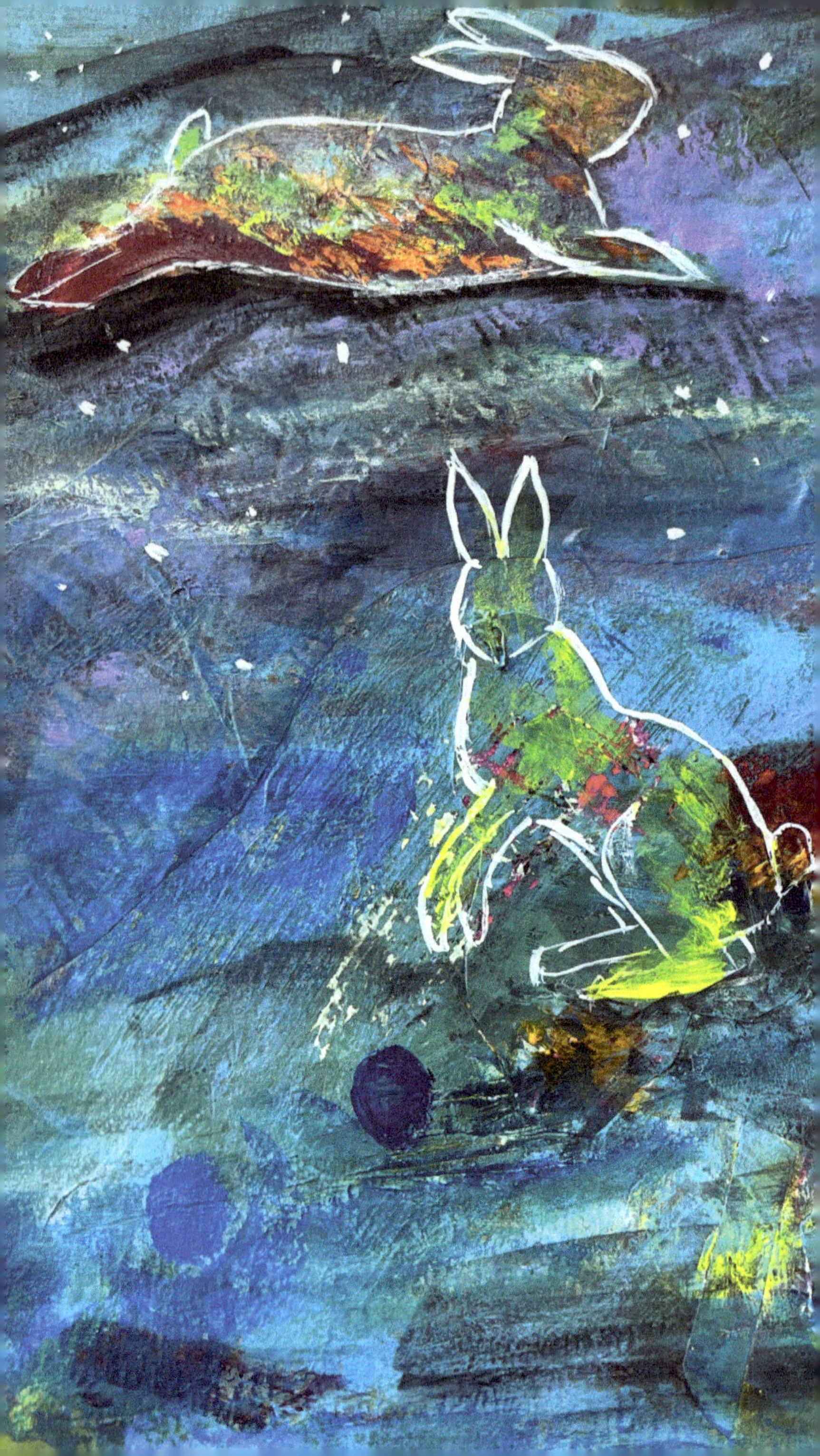

Manifestations

Adornment

Started at 12:29 a.m. and finished at 12:44 a.m.

What adorns you and
sets you apart?
Is it your stellar attitude
and unspoken kindness?
Is it the way you live your life
true to who you are?

Is it your attitude that
shines because you're
not a Debbie Downer
who squashes and quashes
good ideas and fun?

Is your adornment
the way you carry yourself
and stand up for others?
You don't tolerate abuse
or neglect it when it presents

itself in your path.

Is adornment your
ability to get along,
to look out for others
while you take care of
yourself at the same time?

Is your adornment
your radiant smile,
the outward sign
of inward grace,
your expression that
invites others to join in
because you have
nothing to lose?

There's no suspicion,
comparison, shame, or
superiority—but
no inferiority either.

Is your adornment
the ability to feel
into the space and see if
it's your turn to speak?

Is your adornment
the way you navigate conflict,
don't churn the waters and

look for trouble, but don't
back down when you're
called to take a stand?

Is your adornment
your infectious laugh
and buoyant speech
which draws others to you
like a charismatic magnet?
Is your adornment your
winsome style and elegant
storytelling that wraps others in
a cozy blanket of familiarity?

Is your adornment
your vulnerability
and raw willingness
to face and share
the hard stuff in life,
not just the dazzling ways
your life works?

As you refuse to
back down from pain,
stress, and disappointment,
it encourages others and
offers hope that they can be
brave when witnessed
by loving friends.

What you wear on
the outside won't matter
if your inside is unclean
or you are out of integrity.
No outside trappings,
clothes, hats, or jewels
will adorn you like
your bright, colorful,
radiant spirit.

That is your greatest adornment.

Summer

Started at 3:24 a.m. and finished 3:52 a.m.

Summer is a state of mind,
a break from work,
a time for fun and
being a kid again.
Your mood lightens as
the days grow longer.

Some people are sensitive
to light and breathe it in
like the air in their lungs.
Summer's light gives you hope,
warms your spirit, and fills
you with a sense of wellbeing.
More light heralds longer days
when you feel less rushed or
bothered by things you have to do.

Summer offers you

popsicle memories
as you look forward to
playing outside with friends.

You want to ride bikes,
find lost treasure,
swim in the pool, and
splash in the sprinklers.

You love to make
plates of fudge and
play cards for hours
as you listen to music
and daydream together.
You visit relatives and
catch fireflies, which share
their phosphorescent magic
as they become pirate lanterns
and fairy beacons.

Summer allows you to step
away from responsibility,
and create a break in routine.
What are the miracles of summer?
You learn so much from children
if you tune in to their close connection
to nature, joy, and laughter.

Summer is for backyard barbecues
or simple meals, the feeling

of taking your time.
Summer invites you to leave
room for spontaneity and
create spaciousness.
Summer offers late night
walks to the park,
strolls on the beach,
romantic kisses in the moonlight,
or extra time for yourself.

Summer finds you lying like
a lizard on warm flagstone or
sitting in the sun soaking up rays.
In summer, you harvest
vegetables from the garden
or make jam from the fruit trees
in your neighbor's yard.

You take the family camping
and make time for that often-
discussed-but-*never-taken* fishing trip.
The kids have sleepovers and
people linger at family gatherings,
talk, and watch the stars as
they illuminate the night sky.

Summer brings time to be lazy
and slower than your normal pace.
Summer can happen in your mind.
You don't have to wait

for it on the calendar.

You can have a summer soul
when you focus on wellbeing,
warmth, renewal, and nature's bright colors.

If you look, it may be freezing outside.
You might see ice and snow,
but with a little imagination,
you can feel summer as you
journey there in your mind.

The Poems

Started at 6:00 a.m. and finished at 6:08 a.m.

It all starts with a title,
and I know it's time.
At first, I laugh and question
the silly name, outlandish idea,
 or simple subject.
But who am I to question
the wisdom far greater
than my own?

Trusting, willing, and empty
means I am ready to receive
whatever gifts my Higher Power
drops at the doorstep
of my misty mind.

Am I writing about the wind
or a washing machine,
a winged creature or

the way back home?

It's all a journey
as I scamper down
a mysterious path,
cut through a forest,
and wander into a desert.
I make a sharp turn
toward the sea and
boomerang up to
the starry Milky Way.

It's heaven and earth,
nature and nurture,
learning and unlearning,
twisting and somersaulting
through the landscape
of my mind
as I undo all limits
and lift all labels,
which makes me free,
receptive, and
like a child: willing.

Wait

Started at 2:37 a.m. and finished at 2:53 a.m.

Wait.
What do you need
to release before
you forge ahead?
What habits and old ways
can you discard?

Wait.

You can't.
You're called.
You're called now
to wake up,
rise up, and
spread the love.

Wait.
If you wait again,

you still won't
be ready.
You can't wait.
You won't wait.
If you wait, you'll
miss your calling.

Wait, because you
don't know how
or where or why.
Don't waste
another second
with fear, doubts,
negative self-talk,
posturing, or pretending
to know more than others.

You don't need to know,
and it won't help anyway.
The more you
think you know,
the less you do.
When you're empty and
don't need to know,
answers slip in,
hints appear, and
details become clear.

Wait.

You're not sure
what to do, or
how to impress.
You need to meditate
on your intention
and feel with your heart.

What does your soul
yearn to be, do. and
have in this world?
What dreams that
used to hibernate
like bears in a cave
now burst forth from you?

You felt left behind and
unable to catch up.
There's no perfect pace.
No treasure map
guides you; only your
heart and spirit can.

When you explore
with them, you wear
magnetic binoculars
that draw your
destiny to you.
Trust in the
all-knowing eyes
of your true self,

your inner knowing.

Wait.
You're not sure.
Wait.
You don't know.
Wait.
You're scared.

Now is the time.
Your soul calls.

Respond

Started at 3:53 a.m. and finished at 4:07 a.m.

Will you respond
when your soul
urges and nudges you?
Will you respond or
do you sleep
and act complacent?
When your body tells
you to wake up,
pay attention, and
heed a warning,
do you respond?
You receive information
or guidance from above
somewhere in your body.

You may feel it in your gut,
your chest, or your heart.
That's your inner wisdom,

a GPS system that
protects and leads you.

Will you respond when
you feel a sense of unease?
When your body warns you *no*,
do you insist upon *yes*?
How will you respond when
your inner guidance
says not to trust?
Do you ignore it and
override what you receive
because it's awkward,
uncomfortable, or inconvenient?

Will you respond with
joy and enthusiasm
when your body tingles
with electricity and excitement?
Will you say *Yes* to the course,
the job, the lover, or the friend?

When your body flashes
the big green light,
will you be brave and
trust enough to listen,
embrace, and run
with the information?
Will you respond
when you go somewhere

and the vibe changes?
When you know you must go,
will you choose instead to be
polite and refuse to leave?

Sometimes people and
situations change, so you
must be flexible enough
to trust that you can follow
the inner messages
that try to guide you
and keep you out of trouble.

If you tune yourself out,
you'll miss the help or
dismiss it as nonsense.
Decide to respond without
questions or complaints.

Respond and pay attention
to the wisdom that
Spirit offers you.
Respond and you'll
be happy you did
every single time.

Raindrops

Started at 4:06 a.m. and finished at 4:17 a.m.

Raindrops pummel
the ocean as it rushes
toward the shore
in endless waves.

Raindrops splatter
the windshield,
fog the view, and
obscure the landscape.

Raindrops beat upon
the roof and clamor
to be let in as they
ring with impatience.

Raindrops fall
on your face
as your soul breathes

for the first time today.

Raindrops lap
at your heart
as the tenderness
of the moment
overtakes you.

This wet reminder
is a gift from God
of your aliveness,
of your connection to Him.
You desire to be washed
fresh from the cobwebs
of your mind and
how you judge, divide,
and see yourself as higher
or lower than others.

When you let
your mind rule,
you disconnect
from your spirit.
You feel pushed and
rushed like a hamster
that never gets off the wheel.

How did you end up
on the wheel anyway?
You put yourself there

to earn power, praise,
and predictable outcomes,
but you don't need
predictability anymore.

Let the spirit within you
dance with the Divine,
igniting in you a fire of ecstasy.

Let the raindrops come.
They will only refresh.
Nothing can put out your fire now.

Beauty

Started at 2:19 a.m. and finished at 2:43 a.m.

Where is the beauty in your life?
Do you surround yourself with it?
Do you create it?
Your biology pushes you
to seek beauty.
Your soul soars when
you experience it.

Beauty delivers extra energy
as it propels you forward.
It softens a tough situation
and makes your heart melt.
You weep as it sweeps you up
in its glory, and you travel
heavenward as musical
notes wrap around your soul.

The hue of dawn or brashness

of a sunset transports
you to another world.

A wild and riotous carpet of
poppies undulate over
the Tuscan hills, and
deep purple lavender fields
lift your spirit as soft breezes
bring the promise of springtime.

Pristine snowflakes twirl
lightly in the air,
form soft drifts,
and blanket the world
in white perfection.
Winter fairies' paintbrushes
transform bushes with
frost and ice crystals that
create unimaginable lace sparkles.

Beauty can also be a sport
played with skill, determination,
and grit; the magnificence
of a human body as it glides,
leaps, and turns through space.

Beauty is children's kindness,
sharing, laughter, and joy
as they delight in each other
and the world.

Beauty is a couple's love
as it vibrates with
devotion and tenderness.
Beauty is a newborn,
God's perfection in
the promise of new life.

Beauty can be birds
that grace your yard,
bathe in a bird bath,
feast at your feeder,
and sweetly serenade
you from the trees.

Beauty is furry friends,
feathered companions,
and goldfish as they glide
in their aquatic homes.
Beauty is a pet who shares
unconditional love and approval.
Surely pets are your angels.

Whether you experience
beauty in creativity,
Mother Nature, people,
animals, sport, dance, music,
or art, search to uncover
your own beauty within.
There is a place of peace, joy,

and compassion where you
discover a divine spark that
blazes as an ember of
God's love inside your heart.
Tend the flame so that God's
fragment of perfection and
pure love glows within you.
It sustains, enlivens, and inspires
you to add your own special
mark of beauty to the world.

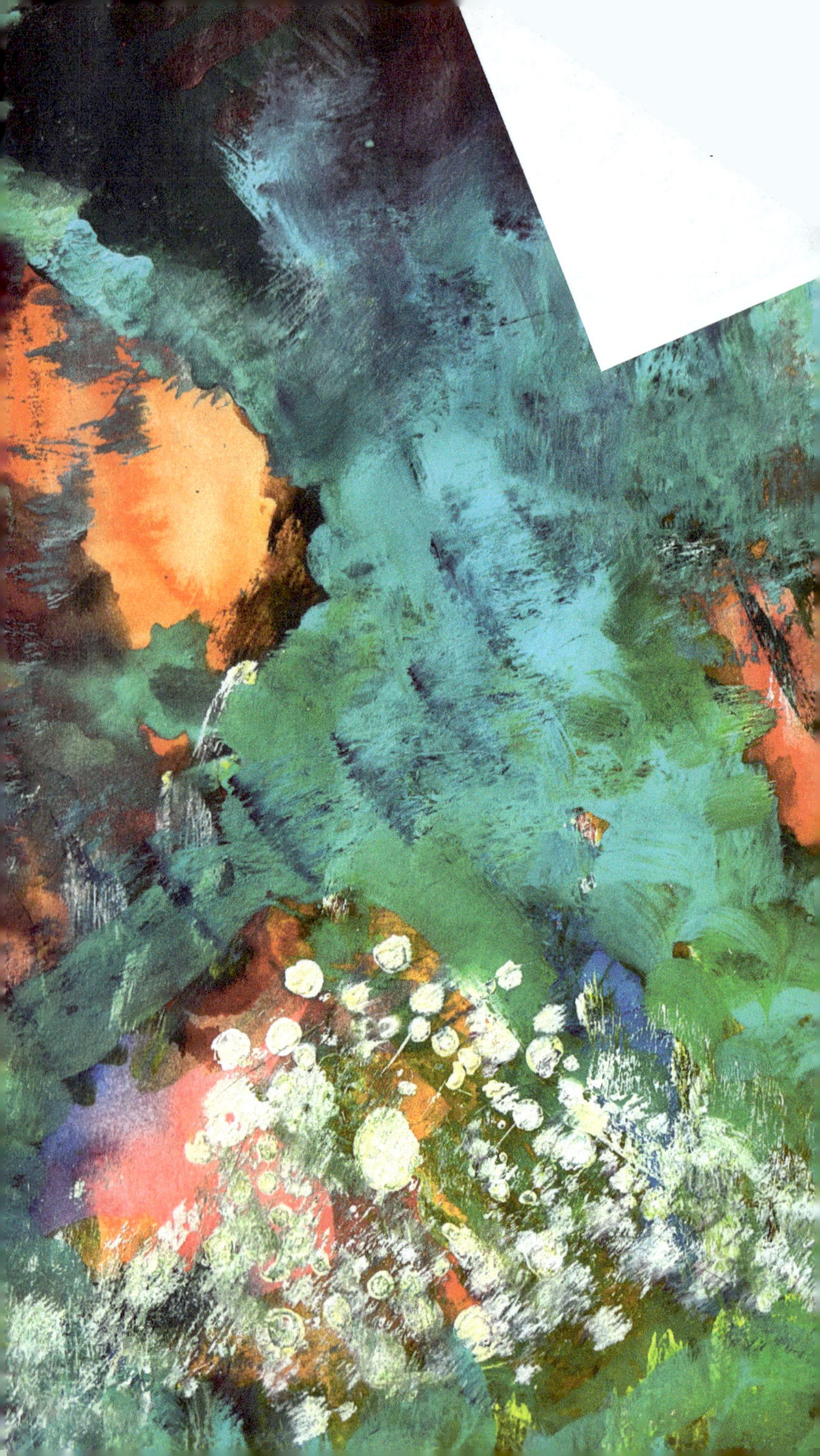

Moorings

Habits

Started at 2:33 a.m. and finished at 3:01 a.m.

What kinds of habits
do you have?
Do you live your life on
autopilot and cruise control?
What kinds of habits make up
your daily grind?
Sometimes we're not aware
of things we do and say.
Books have been written on
changing, cultivating, and breaking
habits, but who cares if you
don't even know what they are?

What happens when you
face a new task?
Do you hesitate and procrastinate,
or do you liberate yourself and
jump right in, not caring

if you're going to be good?

How flexible are you?
Psychologists tell us that the
happiest people bend like trees
in the wind and don't snap off
when things change direction.
Are you moveable?
If so, angels and guides can hint and
whisper ways to make your life easier.

Are your habits ones that support
the lifestyle you choose?
If you say you want to be active,
but you refuse to get off the couch
or away from the computer,
what's out of alignment for you?
If you know you can't control
your behavior and emotions
when you drink too much, but
you're in the habit of turning
to the bottle when times get tough,
how does this habit run your life?
If you say you want to pursue
a fun, creative life, but you
only want to be successful,
you avoid trying what you're
not good at, and your habit
of avoidance and perfection
robs you of discovering

something thrilling about yourself.
If you're in the habit of checking
your phone for texts, news,
or social media every morning
when you wake up, and you want
to create a more positive vibe
in your life, then you miss
the chance to take a breath,
say a prayer, and shower yourself
with peace and possibilities
as you set your intention for the day.
Create your life instead of
inviting the outer world to color
your inner experience.

If you want to learn a foreign language
or hone a new skill, you can't do it
if you only wish it will happen.
You must first decide.
Then commit and choose a small action
that puts your feet on the path
of where you want to be.

Does your decision to learn
something new align
with who you are and what
you really desire?

If you say you're too tired,
but you continue to burn the candle

at both ends, no one can help you.
If you say you want to trust yourself,
but you fill your head with experts' opinions,
then the habit of looking outside yourself
prevents you from cultivating trust in self.

If you try to change too many habits,
you can go crazy and feel overwhelmed.
Take a breath, get centered, and
look at your life now.
What is one thing you don't like
or want to change?

The opposite of that points you
in the direction of what
you want to create.
Imagine having a new habit,
and feel your new life.

Memories

Started at 4:07 a.m. and finished at 4:28 a.m.

Are your memories terrifying
ones that keep you up at night
and disturb your sleep?
Bad things, sad things,
and heartbreak happen.

Don't relive the horror
in your mind as you replay
the scary scenes again.
Walk out of the movie theater
of your mind—or change the channel.

You get into trouble when
you stay in the past or spend
all your time in the future.
You forget that you only have now.

Now is the present moment,

the *here you are* in your life.
What are you doing to
create great memories
for yourself right now?

Don't wish away the minutes
and hours of every day
because you can't tell
how to use them.
Life is a cornucopia of choices.
When you choose,
you create memories.

Life's treasure chest is
chock full of jewels.
Which experience do you wear today?
The fire opal of creativity,
the blue sapphire of public speaking,
or the diamond of performing
and sparkling on stage?

Maybe your stage is a virtual one,
but you can still find
an avenue to share
your shimmering talent.

Do you wear the red ruby
of grounding yourself,
the topaz of friendship,
the aquamarine of new love,

or the pearl of romance?

Do you wear the amethyst of spirituality,
as you study and learn things
about your consciousness?
Do you adorn your hair with emeralds
as you extend your heart, love,
and compassion for others?
Is your necklace a clear peridot,
which reminds you of spring and self-love?

Whatever gems you select from
the treasure chest of activities,
each one represents your choices,
and with each decision you make,
avenues open up for you to
create lasting memories.
The choice is up to you.

If you want to craft a life with
bubbly memories bursting with
laughter, love, joy, and peace,
choose your activities carefully.
Select your friends with wisdom.
You are the magician of your life.
You are no one's victim.

What did you come here to create?
Your actions and inactions determine your story.
Your story determines your memories.

When you dig through the treasure chest,
look for the gold, select some silver and platinum.
Pick the jewels of your experiences
as you are drawn to their color vibrations.
Adorn yourself simply or with every
experience and jewel you want.
After all, you are the memory maker,
and you are beautiful.

True

Started at 4:38 a.m. and finished at 4:48 a.m.

Will you be true to yourself?
Will you heed the warnings
of your soul to give in,
get away, or just goof off?

Will you be true to yourself?
Will you honor yourself,
give your body rest,
feed yourself well
and hydrate too?
These are simple ways
you can be true to yourself.

Are you true about what
you want to do and how
you want to spend your time?
Are you true to crafting
a creative life for yourself,

an outlet where your
soul can grow, learn,
relax, and rest?

Are you true if you listen and learn?
Do you need to play more or just
take some time to be quiet so
you'll really know what being
true to yourself feels like?

Are you true to your friends
and family members by
being loyal to yourself?
Do you set boundaries and
enjoy each other because you
put yourself first instead of
always putting others there?

Are you true with how you
choose to spend your time?
Are you true to what you want
to read, study, and explore?
Are you true to yourself by
taking time to find an oasis within?

The truer you are to yourself
and the more you listen deeply
with your heart about how to live,
the happier you will be.
When you're true to *you*, you'll

find it easier to be true to others. Pure, clear energy permeates your whole being, and because you're in alignment, you'll be true to yourself, which encourages others to be true too.

Resist

Started at 5:10 a.m. and finished at 5:20 a.m.

Resist the urge to direct traffic
or the need to be certain.
Resist, for there isn't any certainty.

Resist laziness, for it is all around you.
Resist the demands of others,
for many pull you off your path
and disturb your appointment with self.

Resist the urge to plan too much or
program your life so there are
no spaces for the creativity to creep in.

If you're always in motion
and full of emotion,
the Creativity Queen may not
have a chance to be seen, felt, or heard.

When you were younger,
you always made time to create.
That was all you knew.
You thrilled over a leaf or rock and
could make anything into something else.

Your imagination peopled the world
with cowboys and castles,
princesses and dragons,
dangers and escapades.
You had countless adventures,
and you had so much fun.

You listened to yourself.
Every waking minute was not filled
with struggling and striving
but with music and merriment.

Resist the urge to let someone else's
creativity steal yours away from you.
It is your birthright, so resist.

Resist the temptation to do nothing
and hope someone else answers a call
from the Muse because you were too tired
or too preoccupied to respond.

Resist the obstacles, excuses, laziness,
and lack of knowing what it will be.
Resist all this and fall deeply, fully,

and joyously into yourself.

Celebrity

Started at 4:39 a.m. and finished at 4:58 a.m.

Do you want to be a celebrity?
What's in it for you?
Why the urge?
Do you want the adulation of crowds,
press of the paparazzi,
television shots, and social media hits?

What do you think fame and fortune
bring you that you can't get yourself?
Do you long to be admired
and uplifted by the masses?
Would you know what to do if that happened?
What do you *really* want?

Ask yourself again.
Why would you want
to be a celebrity?
Is it the love and

acceptance of strangers?
Is it the feeling that
once you're known,
you'll feel better about yourself?

Nothing fills the hole
in your heart or
longing in your soul
except reconnection
with God or Source.

Everyone is born with
the need to find meaning
and purpose in life.
Why are you here?
What are you to do?
Why do you even matter?
The deep longing is the
need to reconnect with your
Higher Self and reunite
with your Maker in the
quiet depths of your Soul.
Will being a celebrity bring you that?

If that's your true calling
and your destiny and
you crave it with every
fiber of your being,
then that is different.
If that's your

heart's desire without
a shadow of a doubt—the deepest
longing of your heart—
you might become
most famous celebrity ever.

But is that what you really want?

Many times you don't
know what you want.
You *think* you do.
Your head talks about it
and you sound lofty
and important.
You might even convince yourself,
but will others feel your passion
and your commitment?

People love stories,
connection, and communication.
Tribal elders sat around fires
and shared their ancestors' wisdom
with messages, stones, and symbols.
Emotion and mystery reigned.
Where is the medicine in your message?

Will people feel drawn to you?
Will they yearn to share your
information or create their own,
or will you just be another

dusty book on a shelf and
remain unopened and unknown
because people can't figure out
why you wrote it in the first place?
People want the genuine you.

What do you offer that
resonates with others,
inspires them, stretches them, and
invites them to step into greatness?

You say you're afraid of failure,
but you may fear being known.
Get out there and shine your light.
The world needs your brilliance.
Maybe you'll become a celebrity,
and if you do, you might
encourage others as well.

Radio

Started at 12:17 a.m. and finished at 12:37 a.m.

What kind of radio receiver are you?
Are you a clear channel easy to receive?
Are you stuck down low only
picking up the *AM* band?
Just because you can't hear doesn't mean
that other stations aren't playing.
There are so many songs
blasting out there now,
but you may just think there's only one.

What does it take to pick up those tunes?
How do you know you're receiving?
Are you willing, ready, empty, open, and free?
If your broadband is narrow,
you'll never hear the Yo-Yo Ma,
Mozart, Bach, rock n' roll,
hip hop, acoustic, or R&B.

What about the standards:
jazz ballads, Broadway tunes,
K-pop, luscious Latin dance tunes,
heavy metal, or alternative?

It's all playing.
There's something for each of us,
and you may miss it all.
You may miss the music
because you aren't ready.

You must stop to breathe.
Your channel is so filled with anxiety
and fear that you block messages
and music trying to get through.

You didn't create enough empty space within.
Your tight jaw closes off expression.
Your throat chakra clamps shut
and nothing comes out.

Open your jaw and create an airway.
become a receiver,
and get ready for the magic.
Just because you can't hear,
doesn't mean it's not happening.
All around you is glorious sound.
Slow down, make space, breathe,
relax, smile, and expect.

Join in the experience.
Expand your broadband.
Go out in nature and listen
to every bird song,
the falling leaves,
the whirl of snowflakes,
soft waves lapping the ocean's edge,
the rushing gurgle of a brook as
it trips across rocks in a stream,
the hot sun crackling off the desert plants,
and the sound of little animals
scuttering and scampering to and fro.

All those sounds are for
your pleasure and delight.
How many sounds do you miss
because your mind is too cluttered
with thoughts, worries, and
preconceived notions about
how you're supposed to hear?

All those natural sounds allow you
to fine tune the radio receiver
and expand the range.
What wonderful music and
messages have you been missing?
When you know how to tune in to
your radio, you'll hear it all.

Free

Started at 3:59 a.m. and finished at 4:10 a.m.

Will you allow
yourself to be free?
Are you ready to step
into magnificence and glory?
Will you clothe yourself
in the rich colors of
acceptance and self-love?

Are you free from
false pride, pretending,
avoiding, excuse-making,
and the torpor of inertia?
Are you free to express and
create because you can?
Do it for joy of the journey,
for beauty, art, poetry,
design, dance, and sweet melodies.
Creativity thrills your soul.

The more you play,
the more you receive.
The more you receive,
the more you can give.
The more you give,
the happier you'll be.

Then you and the receivers
will spread love around,
and you'll all be free.

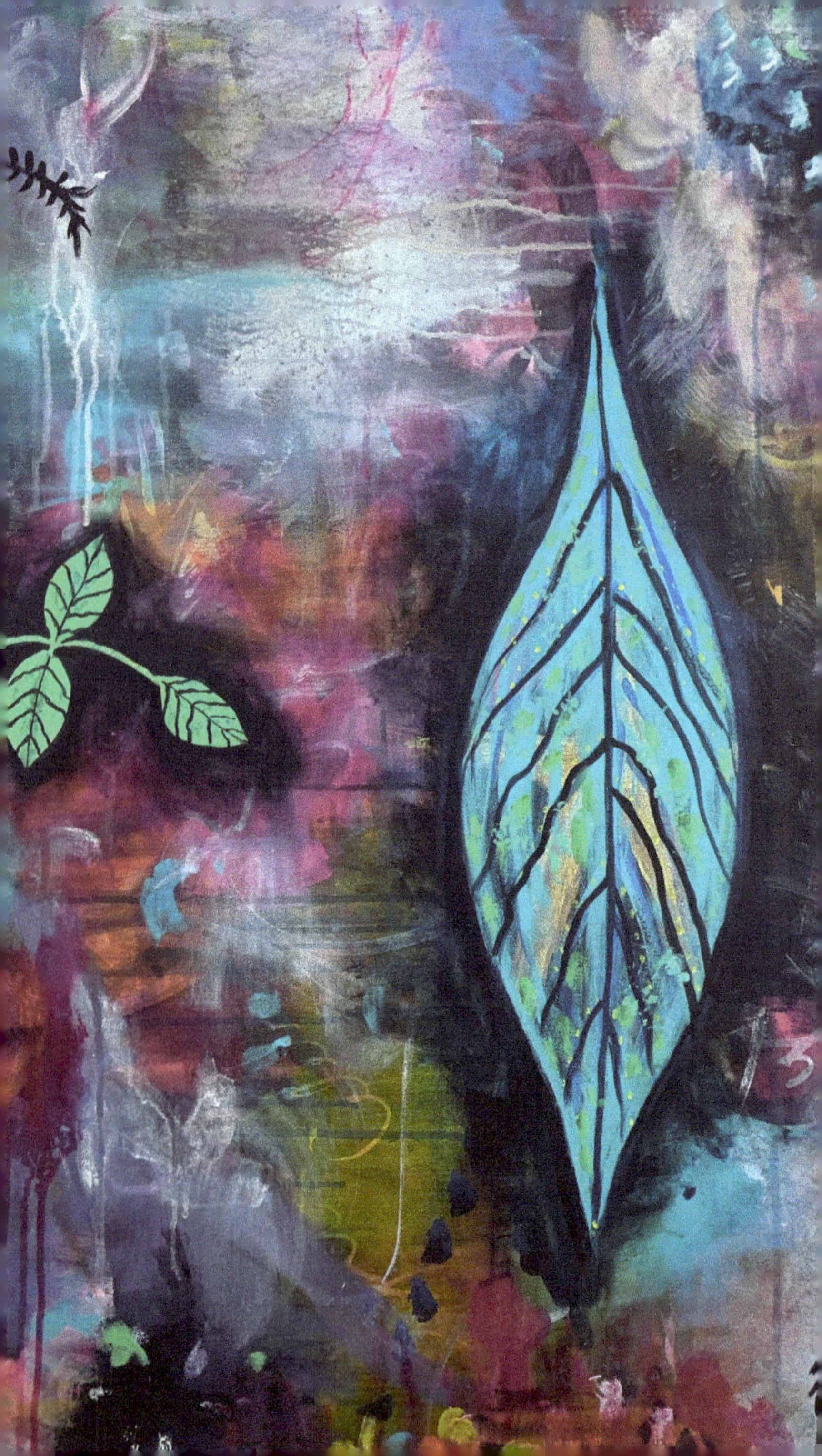

Memories

Intensity

Started at 1:56 a.m. and finished at 2:19 a.m.

What is it like to live
with intensity?
Do you live with purpose?
Do you live *full out?*

Intensity means you're
full out and *full in.*
No lukewarm, toe in the water,
tentative kind of timidity.

Intensity means you
sing with abandon,
unleash your soul,
open your throat chakra,
and free your vocal body.

Intensity is when you paint
with all your senses.

You play music with
the melody ringing
in your head,
and rhythm pulsing
throughout your body.

Senses heighten,
colors buzz with aliveness,
interact with you,
and layer themselves on the canvas
led by spirit's dance of creativity.

Intensity engages body,
mind, and spirit.
Work out, run, lift weights,
do yoga, or hone your sport..
Intensity means you give
your all, and do your best.

It means you decide and
commit, honor, dedicate, and
devote your love and inspiration to
a project, passion, or purpose.

Intensity gets things done
because there's no room for
excuses and no place for sloth.
Intensity intimidates some
and puts off others.

Intensity means you're
in touch with yourself
and can take a break,
breathe, and laugh
because you know that
levity creates space
to expand and play and not
take yourself too seriously.

From this spacious place,
your creativity soars,
new ideas tumble in,
and grace balances intensity.

Rediscover

Started at 2:45 a.m. and finished at 3:21 a.m.

Rediscover the gift of life
by having fresh eyes
with which to see.

Rediscover the joy of learning
when you allow yourself
to have a *beginner's mind.*

Rediscover the thrill of a day
when you cultivate the practice
of gratitude in your life.

Rediscover the freshness
of a relationship when
you become curious
about someone rather
than think you
know everything.

Rediscover the pleasure
of being in someone's company
when you ask for what you want
without demanding it or
assuming the other person
should know what you need.

Rediscover yourself and get out
of the bad neighborhood of
gossip and rumor mongering.
Rediscover the sweetness of
crafting a day that lifts
your spirit and allows you
to feel nurtured, loved,
and attended to because
you journeyed within
to see what you could create.

Rediscover your inner child
as you examine what you
loved as a little one.
Did you organize
the others in games?
Did you write clues
for a scavenger hunt?
Did you play dress up
and put on shows for
anyone who would watch?

Did you cure your
stuffed animal patients
or sketch and doodle
to occupy your time?

Did you lose yourself in books?
Did you sing about everything
as you sat on the front steps
of your house?
Did you explore the neighborhood,
and collect rocks, leaves, or bugs?

Did you run non-stop night and day?
Did you sit on the sidelines
and observe until you could
figure things out while others
ran around being busy?

Did you play in the garden
with the flower fairies
and make homes and play spaces
for them out of your imagination?
Did you take things apart
because of your insatiable desire
to understand how things worked
and see if you could reassemble them?

Did you feel everything going on
around you and withdraw
to come back to yourself?

Did you entertain friends
and family with magic tricks
or surprise your mom or dad
with fresh pancakes and
coffee for breakfast?
Did your parent let you
play in the kitchen
and mix all the spices so
you could become a chef?

As a child, you knew what
lit you up and gave you joy.
You spent hours dancing
in your room or you
created new fashion
for paper dolls by coloring
with a stencil set; now
rediscover your spark.

When you lose yourself in
adult responsibilities of
family, work, home, and
grown-up things you
think are important,
do yourself a favor and
rediscover what thrilled
you as a young person.

If you were the guy
who loved Halloween

and couldn't wait to plan
next year's costume while
you barely touched your stash
of Halloween candy,
maybe now you want to
join friends at Comic Con
or visit sick kids in the hospital
as a superhero.

If you're the girl who
organized her toys
and clothes and wanted
to do the same for others,
maybe you can become a
professional organizer.

Whatever it is that grounded
you, sparked your creativity,
and allowed you to be swept away
for hours in flow,
rediscover that lost part
of yourself.

You will think you've won
the biggest prize ever—
and you have.
You rediscovered yourself
and nothing can hold
you back now.

Wheels

Started at 5:33 a.m. and finished at 5:42 a.m.

Where do the wheels
in your life take you?
Do they roll gently
down the road as
you take in the view,
enjoy the scenery,
breathe in the peace you feel
at that pace,
or do you barrel
down the road
and careen out of control
toward a destiny
you no longer desire?

Are your wheels like
the ones on roller blades
that take you down the sidewalk,
and give you time to race

when you want or glide
like an ice skater if you
feel elegant and slow?
Do the wheels in your life
turn and drive you
down a highway upon which
you don't want to travel?

Does someone else in your life
control your wheels?
They don't know where you
want to go, what you want
to do, or how you like to travel.

What happened to your wheels?
Are they rusty and road-worn,
greasy with boredom, or
shut up in the garage and
neglected so you're not sure
they will ever roll again?

Take out your wheels
and cruise again.
The motion feels fantastic,
and creativity springboards
you out of your doldrum.
Free the wheels of your mind,
so your heart can
go on a vacation.

Wind

Started at 6:47 a.m. and finished at 7:01 a.m.

Wind is a powerful element.
You can hear as it howls over the plains
or whistles through the trees.
Wind is powerful, noisy, and disruptive at times.
It can whip your hair into a frenzy
or ruffle your feathers and cause you
to feel out of control and moody.
Wind is ever present in West Texas.
It can bite through your clothes,
and blow you across the street.
It clears leaves out of your yard
and deposits them somewhere
down the street.
It can drive you crazy with
its incessant roar or steady hum.
Wind tosses clothes
around on the line.
It moves real estate

as it picks up your top soil
and takes it to your
neighbor across the way.

Wind can be gentle in spring,
as it whispers in your ear.
It rustles soft grasses, and it
creates a magic dance
through the wildflowers.

Wind can toss ships at sea
or be the necessary power for a
sailboat as it glides across the lake.
Wind can whip the sea
into a foaming frenzy,
crash waves against boulders,
and pound the shore.
Wind turns windmills and turbines,
and provides power from Mother Nature.

Wind is a force that can wreck things
or create a soft mood.
It can blow a wildfire out of control
or cool you on a hot, sweltering day.
As with many things,
wind's usefulness,
beauty, and definition lie
in the eye of the beholder.
What's your perspective?

Paper Trail

Started at 3:33 a.m. and finished at 3:46 a.m.

What kind of paper trail
do you leave in your life?
What reactions to others
create a paper trail?

Do they know you for your kind
verbal caresses, encouragement,
and support, or do they
remember you as the negative one
for whom nothing is right?

Are you the one who cheers
others on with a sweet smile
and curious attitude?
Do others appreciate that you
see them and acknowledge
their bright spirits, or do
you treat them as inconveniences

or stepping stones to your goals?

Do people say you're the one
who looks them in the eye
and really knows them?
You don't pass by as if they don't exist.

Are you the one who tries
to understand them when they
can't understand themselves?

Do you run and hide from their tears
and neediness, or do you respond
as well as you can?
Do you decide to suspend judgment
even though their actions
make no sense to you at all?

Do you look for ways you might
be the same as others
instead of finding every
difference you can?
You never know someone's story
unless that person shares it.
Your perceptions reflect limited
knowledge and experiences.
What if you don't judge but
instead give everyone the
benefit of the doubt?
What if you treat them *better* than

the way you want to be treated?
If you do that, what a paper trail
you will leave.

The Soda Fountain

Started at 12:22 a.m. and finished at 12:40 a.m.

The soda fountain is
like a drive-through
for your taste buds: a rare treat,
an uncommon experience.
How do you approach
things that are unknown?
Do you look forward
with great anticipation?
Do you wonder and feel joyful?
Does trepidation fill your soul?

What if you are afraid of change?
What do you think happens
if you try something novel?
Can you be excited?
Will you allow yourself to feel

the rush of adrenaline
and pure joy of letting go
like young children who
slide down a snowy slope
or ice skaters who set out
to explore and don't care
where they go?
Can you approach adventure
with innocence and
your eyes wide open?
Can you race down
a sidewalk on your skates
or jump on a trampoline?
Can you take your feet
off the ground to ride
a bike though you're
not sure you can balance?

Will you try a dance step,
kick a ball, pick up crayons
or paints and not care
which color you use?

What if the perfect color
jumps into your hand
and with wild abandon
you throw your heart
and soul onto the
blank paper with
freedom and hope?

No reason, no planning,
just the pure, unadulterated
joy of making a mark
as you thrill in the result,
no matter what?

What if, like the
fizz and bubbles of
a soda fountain drink,
you slurp up life?
You boldly drink it down
and throw caution to the wind?

You don't care about
the end result, but you
want to taste it all,
have it all, and feel it all
like the cold winter wind
that wakes up your face
and the intoxicating scent
of old-fashioned roses
that fill your nostrils with
the sweetest perfume.
Like the sun that bakes
your body as you dig your toes
in the sand while you
lie at the ocean's edge?

What if you plunge into
the surf with laughter and joy

and don't care what you look like
or what others might think,
but you hurl yourself through
the foamy surf, galloping
like a young colt?

What if all that life holds
can be full of surprise,
refreshment, and joy
just like a new drink
at the soda fountain?

Warmth

Started at 7:45 a.m. and finished at 7:57 a.m.

Do you love the warmth
of a spring day?

The warmth of the sun
on your face while clouds form
patterns on a palette of blue?

Do you love the warmth
on your body as you lie on a beach
stretched out on a towel?

Do you love the warmth
from a fire crackling in
the fireplace as it fills
your eyes with wonder while
flames dance and dart around?

Do you love the warmth

of a hand reaching for yours
as you walk in the park?

Do you love the warmth
of children's bodies
pressed gently to you
as you pick them up?

Do you love the warmth
of a blanket, a heavy, weighted one
that covers you as you sit and
try to be still in your meditation chair?

Do you love the warmth
of your friend's smile as
she sees you and her warmth
fills your heart as
she beams her light your way?

Do you love the warmth
you feel in your lover's arms as you
share a soft embrace or deep kiss?
Do you love the warmth
of his body next to yours
as you tumble into bed together?

Do you love the warmth from the
nuzzle of your special animal friend,
the companion who greets you with love
and understands you without words?

Do you love the warmth
in your heart when you complete
a project, pass a test, finish a novel,
or create something special?

Do you love the warmth of belonging,
having friends, understanding,
and being understood?

Warmth, by itself, is great,
and it's even better
when you share it.

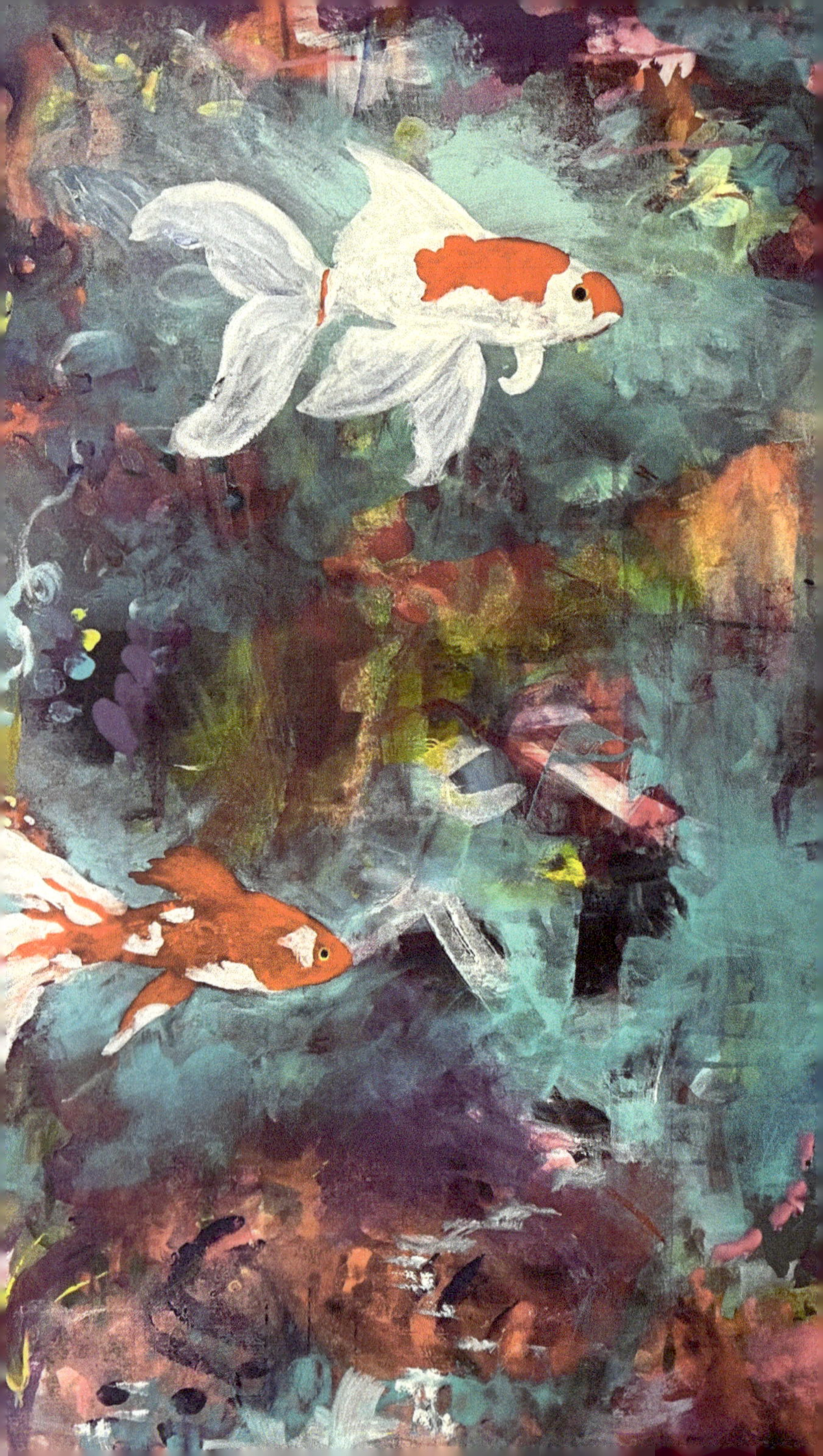

Miracles

Ribbons

Started at 5:24 a.m. and finished at 5:35 a.m.

Ribbons of delight spin
through the crowd
as you move forward.
Where are you going?
What are you doing?
What do you celebrate?

Ribbons of bright,
happy colors adorn
the packages, thrill the givers,
and excite the recipients.

Ribbons of laughter
echo through the halls
as young children scamper
to their classrooms.

Ribbons of light burst forth

from the storm as the
wind changes direction,
and you shiver in the cold.

Ribbons of green and yellow
undulate across the sky
in the rhythmic ritual
of the Northern Lights.

Ribbons can be colors, lights,
gifts, laughter, and decor.
Which one is the real ribbon?
You get to decide.

Don't let someone else
tell you how to define anything.
Use your own words,
descriptions, and meanings.
Let creativity guide you.
You may discover a new meaning
for ribbons that didn't even exist.

Ask for Help

Started at 5:30 a.m. and finished at 5:44 a.m.

Help is always there, but
sometimes you must call for it.
We're not really designed to
do life by ourselves.

Remember that we're
part of love, and love
lives in us, too.
When we put on the cloak
of God, we're clothed
in love and patience,
help and protection.

Help can come in many forms:
the call from a friend
at the moment you
feel lonely or afraid,
a letter or email with news

you've been waiting for,
the loan approval,
the application acceptance,
the money is being sent.

Help can come in subtle ways
or through the words of another.
You can ask for help from angels and
guides, Jesus or Mary, Saints or self.
You don't need to suffer by yourself.
If you feel lonely, afraid, worried
or distraught, reach out.
Are you available when
someone else needs help?
You can receive help, and
you can extend assistance.

Help is rewarding and allows you
to feel connected to others.
You don't have to do it all
by yourself, but most people
don't read minds.
Realize that you don't
have to fly solo.

Just as one musician can
play a note and entertain,
the music grows richer and
more complex as you layer
in different sounds.

Whether it's choral music,
a symphonic piece, or
a smooth set of jazz,
once you add in the other
elements, the melody crescendos
in magnificence and mellifluence.
That will happen to you, too,
as you reach out and ask for help
instead of stumbling down
a lonely path by yourself.

Celebration

Started at 5:04 a.m. and finished at 5:20 a.m.

Where's the celebration
in your life?
Do you invite others
to the party
or is this an
affair for one?

What's the reason
for the celebration?
How do you connect
with the miracle
of your own life?

You are here to
live, grow, flourish,
create, share, teach,
learn, and be thankful for
the next life-sustaining breath.

Do you celebrate the
beauty all around you:
the colorful birds who
feed outside the window;
the quiet peace of dawn
as the world wakes up;

the morning sunrise
as it paints the sky;
the bold streaks of sunset
as they tint the western horizon;
the crystal stars that sparkle
like celestial diamonds;

the big drifts of snow
and ice crystals that
magically drape from
trees like the dripping fingers
of a mysterious snow queen;

the rolling green hills of Tuscany in
fifteen shades of gold and green;
the windswept plains or
craggy mountains as their peaks
rise to the heavens;

the majesty of the sea as
it crashes against the rocks;
the continual waves

as they return time and again
to the shore;

the riot of colorful flowers
in your garden at springtime;
a mystical walk through
the woods as trees reach out
to support you and share
their life-giving oxygen
and soul-giving wisdom?

In addition to beauty, do you
want to celebrate a child, job,
friend, or challenge that you meet
or obstacle you overcome?
What about the play you write?
The dance you choreograph,
the painting you create,
the mile you run, or
the yoga pose you
can finally hold?
Does the foreign language you
master or the retreat
you design inspire
others to try something new?

Your special moments
call for celebration,
both the big ones and
the small ones.

What do you need to celebrate
today, and how can a celebration
of life, yourself, and your triumphs
help others realize you don't have
to wait for a big occasion?

You can have your celebration now.
What are you waiting for,
an invitation?
That only comes from you.

The Washing Machine

Started at 2:08 a.m. and finished at 2:33 a.m.

What does a washing machine do?
It's an agitator that tosses our clothes
and swishes them in the water to
make us presentable once more.

Do we need to be churned
and turned upside down?
Washed clean from our grimy ways?
Are we stained and soiled, wrinkled
and care-worn, looking to be brightened,
whitened, and generally refreshed?

What about our weary spirits?
Like our clothes, do they need a clean rinse
from our habitual negativity, critical
self-talk, and gossiping tongues?

Do we long to be made clean
and new in our attitudes?
Are we dirty from judgments and
preconceived notions, the impatience
and impertinence of our ego-driven selves?

Will a washing machine do enough for us,
or must we search for new products?
Will bleaches, liquids, and stain removers
do the job, or do we need an old-fashioned
way of rubbing ourselves spotless on the
water-covered rocks in nature?

What if a fancy liquid and the newest machine
won't remove the filthiest parts of us?
What if we have to be our own washing machines
and look for new ways to refresh ourselves?

Will sitting in the sun, hearing the morning call
of the dove, or walking barefoot on the hillside
restore us to wholeness?

Mother Earth herself can wash us
with life-giving beauty and heart:
the freshness of the breeze,
the ripple of flowers in the wind,
the soft snowflakes that brush our lashes,
the massive oak that sheds leaves
as it creates a display of branches

that reach heavenward in a tribal dance.

The brilliant pink sky and purple streaks,
the blast of orange and splotches of blue,
sunsets thrill us with color combinations
that morph as clouds transform,
golden hues and softened tones
give way to the dark, and
stars twinkle and sparkle
like diamonds as evening
deepens to inky black,
the glory of the moonlight as
it envelops us in softened rays.

You must slow down and take a breath.
Breathe in all the beauty while you can.
Search your eyes for the life-sustaining
calling cards of nature that clean us
deep down while our souls drink from the
ever-changing intoxicating beauty of the earth.

It is here that we will be made clean,
our spirits purified from griminess,
our lungs filled with life-giving oxygen
which gives us space—space without talking,
judging, or deciding—a moment to notice,
to fill every cell of our bodies with
the freshness of nature,
the eternal supplier of renewal.
This way wipes clean our

less-than-perfect selves.
We feel refreshed and renewed.
Who needs a washing machine after all?

Whipped Cream

Started at 1:18 a.m. and finished at 1:31 a.m.

It's the top of the sundae,
the fun, fluffy part.
You pile a creamy delight
high onto pies, cakes,
and ice cream.
It's good by itself or in coffee.

There are a number of
ways to enjoy it.
Do you squirt, pile,
smear, or shape it?
Are you generous or skimpy
with your topping?
A little extra makes
things special and fun.

Where is the whipped cream
in your life?

Do you practice piano
or play soccer with friends?
Do you learn hip hop steps
or excel in photography?
Do you love the roughness of rugby?
Do you fly down the sidewalk
on inline skates?

Do you challenge yourself
in ballet or lose yourself
in a great book?
Do you try a new yoga stretch
or surprise yourself with art?

When you're knotted up
at work, do you treat yourself
to a few deep breaths?
Do you savor a bike ride
when the world bursts out
in a blaze of sunset hues?
Do you skinny dip in a lake or
lie on a beach doing nothing?

Where's your whipped cream?
Do you deny yourself
the sweet stuff?
Are you afraid extra calories
will ruin your disciplined life?
Live a little and add that extra

unnecessary sweetness and
treatness to your life.

Forgo the suffering and
give up the sacrifice.
Be silly, play with your food,
savor your life, and don't
take it all so seriously.
You probably need
a little whipped cream, and
if you're worried about dairy,
try the coconut variety.

What are you waiting for?
Squirt it, spray it, or pile it high.
Add whipped cream to your life.
The extra pleasure brings
a smile to your face
and joy to your heart.
Maybe you just needed a
little sweetness and
some whipped cream.

Do You Care?

Started at 3:08 a.m. and finished at 3:28 a.m.

Do you care what
goes on in your mind
or do you feel
that you have very
little control over it?

Whether you agree or not
or whether you
realize it or not,
you are the thinker
of your thoughts.
You're the one
who creates them.
They originate with you.
Are you aware?
Do you care?

The thoughts in your head

create your reality,
your emotions, your actions.
Do you care?
Did you know that it is you
who must take responsibility
for the life you are living?

Your thoughts are
the originator of it all.
Do you care if
you're mean to yourself?
Do you care if you
misjudge everyone?
Do you care if you
elect your ego to be
in charge of your life
instead of your heart?

Your heart is the wise one.
It sees with compassion
love, and connection.
Do you care that
you give more weight
to your intellect,
and let your mind
be your master?

Do you care that
you miss the opportunity
to know yourself on a deep

and meaningful level?
Do you care that
you fill your day with
such a cacophony of noise
that it challenges you
to hear the soft whispers
of your soul?
Do you care that you
miss the the true desires,
yearnings, and knowing
of your spirit?

If there is no place for
you to meet your spirit,
no quiet resting spot,
no oasis in the desert
of your daily life,
no journaling, no quiet
walks in nature,
no deep breathing or
big stretches of
unplanned time and
space, do you care?

You are not nurturing
the relationship with the
Divine within because
who can meet God when
there's so much chaos going on?

The contemplatives knew
that to honor the relationship
with God within, they
had to have a prayer time
quiet time, a receiving time,
when they would be still,
open, and ready.
They did not have to know.

Do you care that
you might miss the
chance to meet
and greet yourself,
to see what you want,
to know the dreams you spin?
Do you care enough
to make a few changes?
Don't beat yourself up
and then avoid even more
because you're not perfect.
Your inner child doesn't
seek perfection, but wants
time to be seen and heard
and played with.

Do you care that you
ignore your little child?
Your inner child is hungry for
companionship and misses
being your playmate.

Do you care enough
to make these changes?
You don't have to climb
an entire mountain at once.
Just start small, but care
enough to give yourself
the treat *of* yourself.

Renewal

Started at 1:43 a.m. and finished at 2:00 a.m.

Do you refresh at
the waters of yourself?
What needs renewal now?
Do you lose your way in
the labyrinth of life?
Does your life feel stale like
last night's dinner conversation?
Does your soul long for
renewal with the Divine?

Do you step into the
pool of self-reflection?
Are you aware which
habits and outdated ways
must go to allow you
to elevate to a more
evolved sense of self?

What ideas or inner
thoughts need renewal?
Are you forever stuck
in a way that does not
serve you or others?

Does your Spirit
need renewal?
Have you asked yourself
what delights you?
What brings you joy,
what kind of adventure
contributes to renewal
and refreshment?
What invigorates and
inspires you?

Does renewal come
if you drop a group
of friends who pull you back
and don't celebrate your
growth and new ideas?

Does renewal ask how
you can best serve or
does renewal mean
to stop serving so much
and check in to see
what *you* want to do?

Does renewal mean
to remember how grateful
you feel to be alive right now?
Does renewal ask you
to find unique ways
to express yourself?

Does renewal mean
you give yourself permission
to be reborn at the waters
of nothingness,
of doing nothing, being nothing,
and emptying yourself?

You can open yourself to magic,
miracles, and mindfulness.
Maybe doing nothing,
being nothing, and
having nothing—no agenda
and no plan—is the
real secret to renewal.

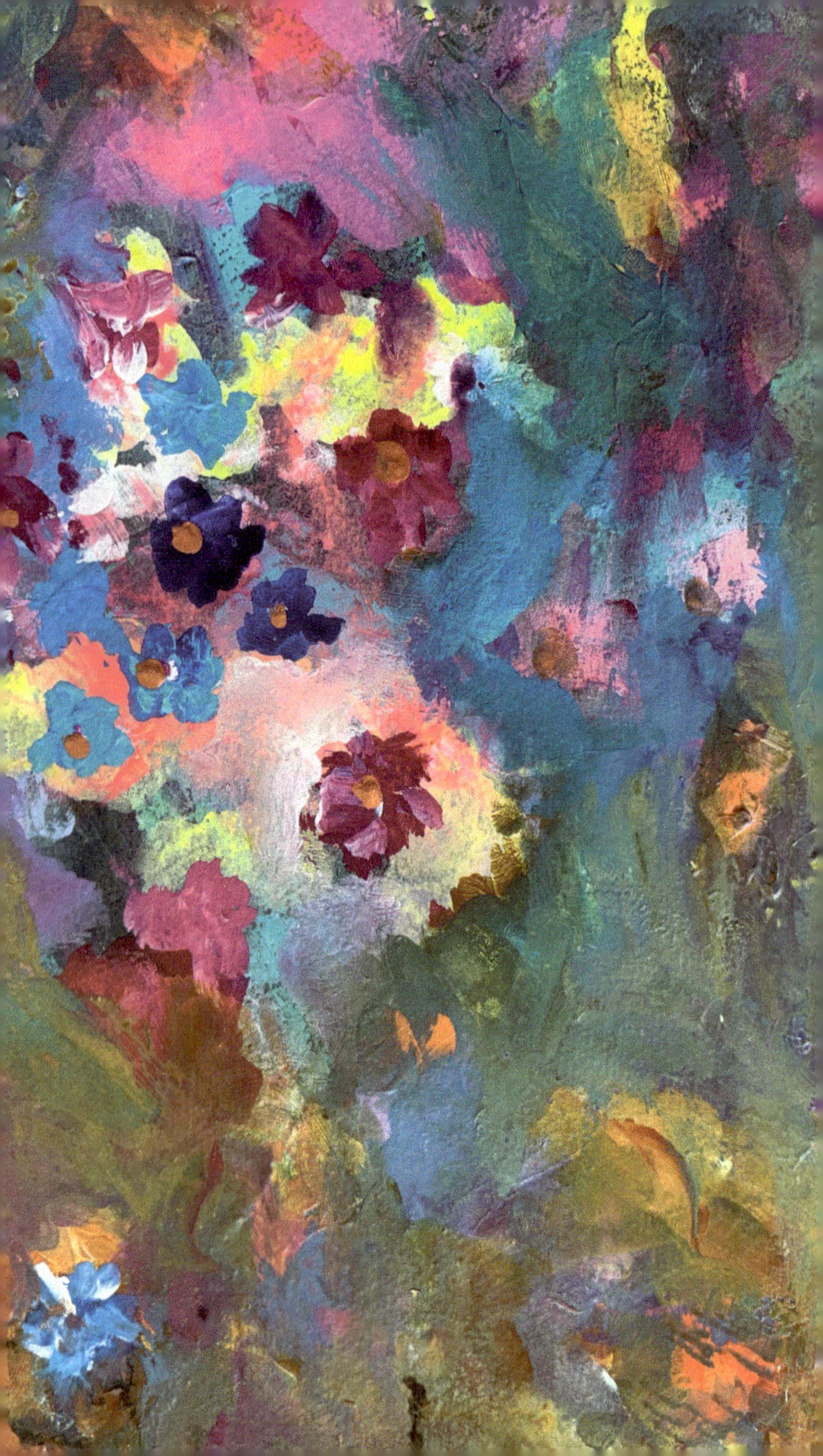

Acknowledgements

I have been inspired by many people over the years, and I first want to acknowledge all of my teachers, especially Sonia Choquette, with whom I have studied since 2010. She is an incredible teacher, mentor, and role model. Sonia challenges her students to grow, and she is generous in sharing her knowledge while being completely authentic in her own evolution. In the early 1980s, I discovered SARK (Susan Ariel Rainbow Kennedy) and was completely enthralled with her bold use of color and deep dive into creativity. I received training from Andrea Hess in reading the Akashic Records, and for that I am grateful. In 2021, I started a year-long journey into *A Course in Miracles* led by Robert and Hollie Holden, which I continue today. Their love, warmth, and sense of community encourages my connection to God and encourages me to express love rather than fear as often as I can.

I am grateful to my publisher Brianne van Reenen, who enthusiastically joined me this summer as we performed in Moonlight Musicals' production of Disney's *Newsies*. In addition to being my publisher and a visionary, Brianne is the owner of the beautiful independent bookshop Wild Lark Books in Lubbock, Texas, where she helps build community and offers wonderful outreach to many writers. Thanks to Heather Dakota for introducing me to the art of editing in *Spirited Poems for Spirited People.* Thanks so much to my current editor Viannah Duncan, who so skillfully edited my poems with great love and care. Thanks to my coach and friend Jennifer Currie, artist and creative, whose compassion, energy work, and skills keep me evolving and growing. Leslie Helpert—friend, voice coach, writer, deep thinker, and wildly creative person—continues to support and inspire me in many ways. Thanks also to my voice teacher Alexa Vogelzang Brown, who helps me express joy in singing. Thanks to all my friends and fellow performers at Moonlight Musicals in Lubbock for giving me an opportunity to share the stage and express our joy in creating live theater. I want to thank Flora Bowley for teaching me to paint boldly on large canvases and to her fellow artist and close friend Lynzee Lynx, who was so loving and encouraging during Flora's painting workshop in Portland, Oregon.

I also want to thank friends from a year-long support group I led connected with Sonia Choquette's course "Your Glorious Life." Thanks to Shannon, Judy, Paz, Kathleen, and especially Kimberly, who eagerly awaited my new poems almost as much as I did. Kimberly was enthusiastic and supportive throughout the entire month I was writing. Thanks to Jordana Borensztajn from Australia, who was in a small mentoring group led by Sonia Choquette. Jordana's great sense of humor and light-hearted joy remind me not to take myself too seriously. I also want to acknowledge Rebecca Campbell, Hay House author and good friend, along with other students of Sonia Choquette—Monika Laschkolnig, Susanne Snellman, Fiona Radman, and Sanja Plavljanic-Sirola—who shared their dreams with me in an international mastermind group. Thanks to Leland Arnsdorff, who attended Sonia's training with me and has always championed my creative endeavors.

A huge thanks to Bonnie Hill, coaching colleague and fantastically nurturing friend who always "gets" me. Everyone needs a friend like Bonnie Hill. Thanks also to Anne Durand, Master Certified Coach, who was my coach and teacher at MentorCoach and gave me an opportunity to be a trainer. Anne encouraged me to get in touch with my intuition before it became a popular topic. Thanks to Carol Solomon, PhD, and Jeff Kaplan, PhD, psychologists and fellow coaches, who helped me develop my skills. Thanks to an amazing group of friends, The Morningstars, who attended a year-long leadership training course through CTI near Santa Rosa, California, with me in 2003. I felt especially supported by my roommate and travel companion Madelyn Roche and by Robert Giambrone, Jim Bower, Phil Hoch, and Anese Cavanaugh. I also wish to thank my friend Susan Ross, who has shared life's journey, especially related to parenting and personal development. Her wisdom and insights have been a gift to me. I want to acknowledge my good friend, colleague, and child psychiatrist John Gelinas, MD, in

Connecticut, who is a force for good and who trusted me with the families he was helping. John has been a constant support and encourager for my creative endeavors while being an artist and author himself, so he understands the value of creative expression on a personal level. I am grateful to all the clients and people who have allowed me into their lives and to the clients I have yet to meet. I also want to give a big thanks to Terri Blassingame, Lubbock friend and reiki master, whose intuition and playfulness bless me.

I want to thank Jake Maxwell, friend and senior pastor at Second Baptist Church in Lubbock, Texas, who sees the spiritual in everything and who is not afraid to think outside the box. I also want to thank Allison Maxwell for taking the photo on this book cover because she captures my joyful spirit. Thanks also to Sarah Herrington, PhD, director of choral studies for Wayland Baptist University, who uses some of the poems from my first book of poetry to encourage and inspire her choral students. I want to acknowledge and thank my friend Joe Rose, who has been supportive of my family throughout the years. Joe is a business leader and an amazing artist, and he took time to encourage me by telling me I had a way with color. Sometimes we don't even realize how one person's witnessing of us can make such a difference in our lives, but Joe's witnessing of me has made a difference in mine.

Thanks to my friend Callie Kostelich, PhD, professor and writing program administrator at Texas Tech

University, who engages me in deep conversation and some of life's most interesting questions. I am indebted to friends Serafina, Theresa, Luisa, Caden, Isabella, Belinda, Samuel, Serena, Clarissa, and Magdalena for their guidance in bringing this poetry to the world. Thanks to my twin sister Bonnie Jump for helping me first organize the poems and also to my sister Gretchen Walker and brother Richard Brown for their support. Thanks so much to my friend, Prisma Brito, who checked my Spanish poem for accuracy and assured me that my translation into English was correct.

I am grateful to my son Chris, daughter Camille, and granddaughter Liesl for their interest in hearing what I have to say. Their opinions matter to me. I am especially thankful for my husband Mark, who is my greatest gift and who loves and encourages me to be myself in all endeavors, large and small. He is my biggest champion. Thanks also to God, my guides, angels, unseen helpers, ancestors, and beings of light who help us all every day in many ways. Thanks to the many people who bought *Spirited Poems for Spirited People* and also to you, new readers, who found *Messages at Midnight.* In advance, I want to express my gratitude to and for you, and I pray that these poems will encourage and inspire you to create the joyous lives you want to live while knowing that you are loved beyond all measure. You make a difference in our world.

About the Author

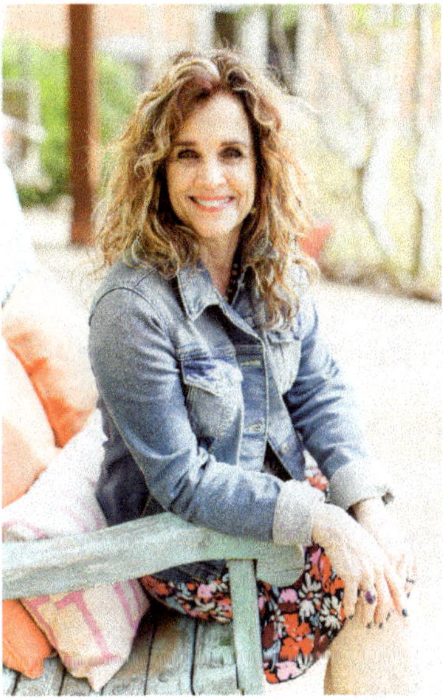

Betsy Bass is a Life Coach, Intuitive Healer, and Creative Spirit. She has more than 40 years combined experience as a Marriage, Family, and Child Therapist and coach. Betsy's love of beauty and dedication to living a vibrant life inspires everything she does. She's multi-lingual, has lived on both coasts and in the middle of the country, enjoys travel, and constantly explores new ways to express her creativity from singing and dancing to painting, drawing, and writing. Since 2014, she has become passionate about performing in musicals. She combines her grounded expertise as a coach with reiki and Akashic

Record wisdom to guide those seeking a deeper connection to their intuition, creative expression, and abundant living. Betsy is very happily married to her husband, Mark, and they live in Lubbock, Texas.

Learn more at www.betsybass.com

Also by Betsy Bass

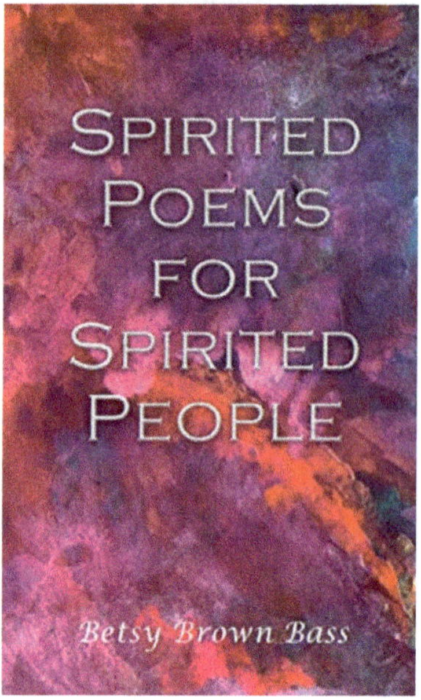

ISBN: 9781955346160

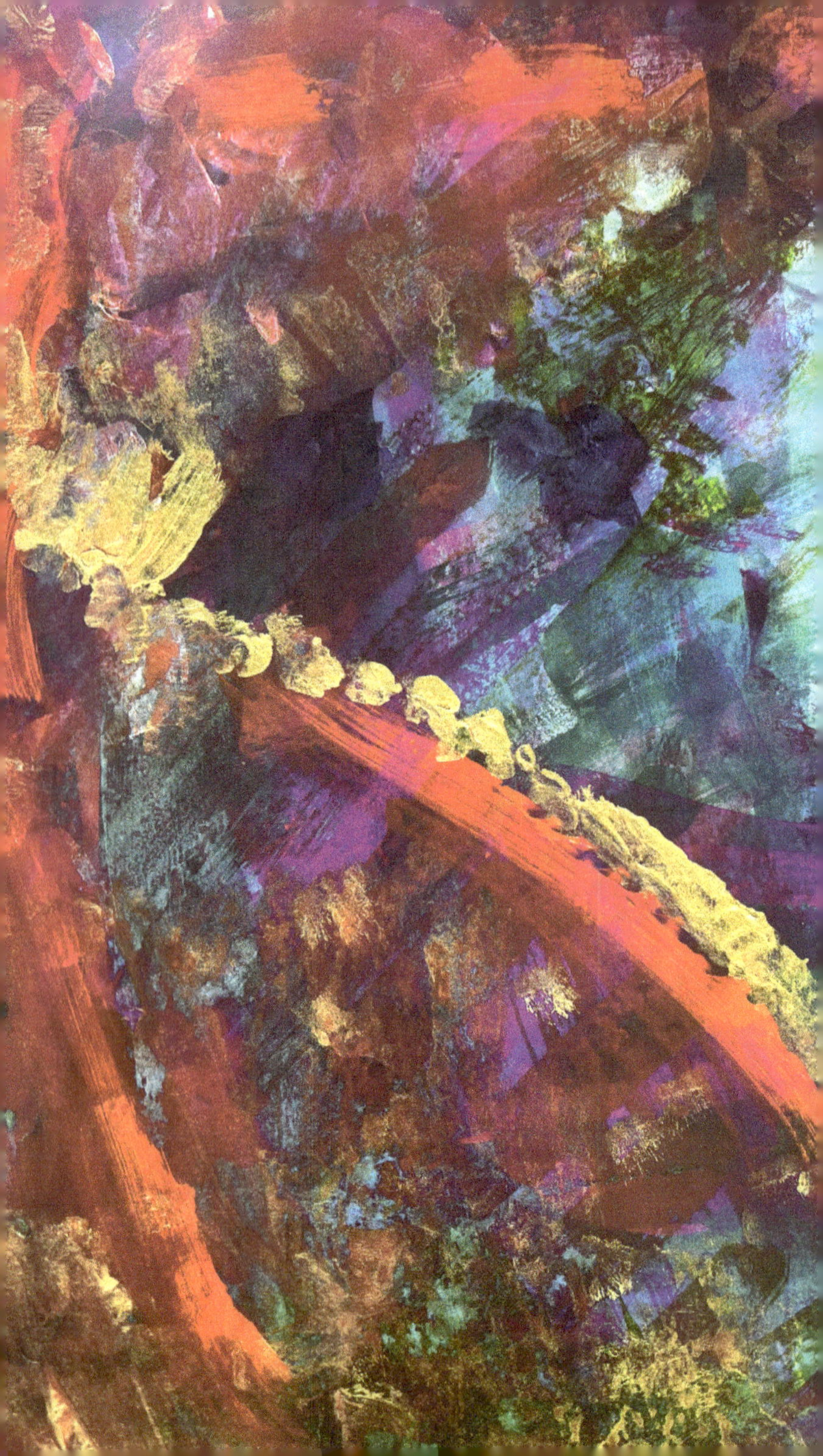

Resources

Note: All @handles are for Instagram.

Sonia Choquette (https://www.soniachoquette.net and @soniachoquette). Membership "Good Vibes Tribe." Spiritual teacher, intuitive mentor, best-selling author and creator of oracle cards and courses. Podcast (Spotify): *It's All Related* with her daughters Sonia and Sabrina.

Sonia Choquette-Tully (https://www.soniatully.com and @soniatully). Mentoring, workshops, co-author of *You Are Amazing* (2017) with sister Sabrina.

Vishen Lakhiani (Founder and CEO of https://www.mindvalley.com and @vishen). *The Code of the Extraordinary Mind* (2016) and *The Buddha and the Badass* (2020).

Brene Brown (https://www.brenebrown.com and @brenebrown) *The Gifts of Imperfection* (2010), *Daring Greatly* (2012), *Rising Strong* (2015), *Braving the Wilderness* (2017), *Dare to Lead* (2018), *Atlas of the Heart* (2021). Podcast (Spotify): *Unlocking Us*.

SARK (Susan Ariel Rainbow Kennedy) (https://www.planetsark.com and @sarkifylife). Artist, author, speaker, teacher.

Samantha Bennett (https://www.TheRealSamBennett.com

and @therealsambennett). *Get it Done: From Procrastination to Creative Genius in 15 Minutes a Day* (2014), *Start Right Where You Are: How Little Changes Can Make a Big Difference for Overwhelmed Procrastinators, Frustrated Overachievers, and Recovering Perfectionists* (2016).

Rebecca Campbell (https://rebeccacampbell.me and @rebeccacamplbell_author). Author, artist, teacher, creator of oracle cards. Podcast (Spotify): *Returning*. The Sanctuary membership site. *Light is the New Black* (2015), *Rise Sister Rise* (2016),

Letters to a Starseed (2021). Founder of The Inner Temple Mystery School.

Lee Harris (https://www.leeharrisenergy.com and @leeharrisenergy). Energy intuitive and transformation guide, musician. Online courses, downloads, and membership site The Portal.

Julia Cameron (https://www.juliacameronlive.com and @juliacameronlive). Teacher, author, artist, composer. *The Artist's Way* (1992), *It's Never Too Late to Begin Again: Discovering Creativity and Meaning at Midlife and Beyond* (2016).

Flora Bowley (https://www.florabowley.com and @florabowley). Artist, author, creative pioneer. *Brave Intuitive Painting* (2012), *Creative Revolution* (2016), *The Art of Aliveness* (2021).

Lynzee Lynx (https://www.yourstrangefriend.com and @lynzeelynx). Artist, jewelry maker, teacher. *Fresh Paint* (2021) written with Flora Bowley.

Leslie Helpert (https://www.dynamicvoicetraining.com and @lesliehelpert). Vocal coach, musician, composer, artist, author.

Robert Holden (https://www.robertholden.com and @drrobert_holden). Author, teacher, psychologist. Hollie Holden (https://www.hollieholden.me and @hollielholdenlove). Artist, teacher, group leader. Robert and Hollie Holden host an annual study of *A Course in Miracles* (www.2022.everydaymiracles.love).

Jennifer Currie (https://www.jennifercurrie.com and @jennifercurrieart). Artist, intuitive coach.

Diana Cooper (https://www.dianacooper.com and @dianacooperangels). Therapist, healer, author, and creator of books and oracle cards.

Kyle Gray (https://www.kylegray.uk and @kylegrayuk). International speaker and author of books and oracle cards.

Colette Baron-Reid (https://www.colettebaronreid.com and @colettebaron_reid). Intuitive counselor, medium, TV personality, Author of books and oracle cards, and radio host.

Marianna Voulgaris (www.trinityherbalsandwellnesscenter.com). Herbalist of herbal wisdom based in: Western herbalism, Ayurveda, Chinese medicine, plant energetics, aromatherapy, planetary herbology). Flower essence therapist, shamanic and medical astrologer, spiritual guide and teacher, yoga instructor, personal trainer and nutrition consultant, owner of Trinity Herbals and Wellness Center. Podcast (Spotify): *Soul Reverence*.

Patty Davis and Judea Lynch (www.spiritspeakerspodcast.com and @spiritspeakerspodcast).

Patty Davis: www.wingandaether.com, Judea Lynch: www.alignandshinekauai.com.

Brianne van Reenen (www.wildlarkstrategies.com and @wildlarkbooks). Publisher, Wild Lark Books.

Paintings by Betsy Bass are titled as follows -
Introduction: *Midnight Sky*
Meditations: *Pink Lotus*

Mirrors: *Mystic Waterfall*
Musings: *Magical Owls*
Manifestations: *Cosmic Bunnies*
Moorings: *Serenity*
Memories: *Midnight Garden*
Miracles: *Fantastic Fish*
Acknowledgments: *Floating Flowers*
Resources: *Rainbow Gold*

Weird

Started at 6:06 a.m. and finished at 6:21 a.m.

Do people call you weird or
do you label yourself this way?
Embrace your weirdness.
Who wants to be exactly like
everyone else anyway?

Perhaps you feel weird because
you chose an unusual career.
Maybe you feel weird because
you listen to your vibes and
follow your intuition.
You do things spontaneously
that don't make sense to others.
Embrace your weirdness.

It keeps you safe,
helps you map
a new direction,
or creates a dream.

Don't worship your mind

and simply follow your intellect.
Feel free to respond to and
follow weird inner urgings.
Your one-of-a-kind GPS
brings you home safely.
Embrace your weirdness.

Do you feel weird because
you follow your heart?
Others can benefit if they
follow in your footsteps.
Do you change your mind
on a whim because of nudges?
How many times do angels
try to help you out?
Do you heed the urge
to call someone,
take an umbrella
even if it's sunny,
grab a spare key,
or walk a different route?

Do you follow inner advice
and feel weird because you
can't explain your
actions to friends?
Embrace your weirdness.

You want to be
loved and accepted.

You don't want others
to judge you or make
you question your sanity.
It's okay not to fit in
all the time.
The more you accept
your God-given uniqueness,
the more you
can accept others.
Celebrate your weirdness.
Wouldn't that be
weird and wonderful?